**THE I**
**INTERNATIONAL**

# THE REAL SPLIT IN THE INTERNATIONAL

**Enlarged edition**

**Theses on the Situationist International
and Its Time, 1972**

Situationist International

Translated by John McHale

Pluto Press

LONDON • STERLING, VIRGINIA

First published as *La Véritable Scission dans L'Internationale* by
Editions Champ Libre, Paris, 1972. Republished with further
appendices by Librairie Arthème Fayard, Paris, 1998.
Edited by Patrick Mosconi.

This edition first published 2003 by Pluto Press
345 Archway Road, London N6 5AA
and 22883 Quicksilver Drive, Sterling, VA 20166-2012, USA

www.plutobooks.com

British Library Cataloguing in Publication Data
A catalogue record for this book is available from the British Library

ISBN   0 7453 2128 3 hardback
ISBN   0 7453 2127 5 paperback

Library of Congress Cataloging-in-Publication Data
Véritable scission dans l'Internationale. English
   The real split in the International : theses on the Situationist
International and its time, 1972 / Situationist International ;
translated by John McHale.
      p. cm.
'First published as La véritable scission dans L'Internationale by
Editions Champ Libre, Paris, 1972'—Verso t.p.
   ISBN 0–7453–2128–3 (hbk) — ISBN 0–7453–2127–5 (pbk)
   1. Internationale situationniste. I. Title: Theses on the
Situationist International and its time, 1972. II. Debord, Guy, 1931–
Theses on the Situationist International. 2003. III. Sanguinetti,
Gianfranco. IV. Internationale situationniste. V. Title.
   HN1.V4513 2003
   303.48'4—dc21

                                                            2003006772


10   9   8   7   6   5   4   3   2   1


Designed and produced for Pluto Press by
Chase Publishing Services, Fortescue, Sidmouth, EX10 9QG
Typeset from disk by Stanford DTP Services, Towcester
Printed and bound in the European Union by
Antony Rowe Ltd, Chippenham and Eastbourne, England

This book is supported by the French Ministry for Foreign Affairs, as part of the Burgess programme, headed for the French Embassy in London by the Institut Français du Royaume-Uni

*Liberté • Égalité • Fraternité*

RÉPUBLIQUE FRANÇAISE

# CONTENTS

# TRANSLATOR'S ACKNOWLEDGEMENTS

I would like to thank Eamon Butterfield, Donald Nicholson-Smith and Alice Debord for their help with this translation. Thanks too go to Anne Beech, Robert Webb, Sophie Richmond and Ray Addicott at Pluto.

*For Alice Debord*

# Introduction

*John McHale*

A key device in the work of both the Letterist and the Situationist Internationals, the *détournements*[1] in *La Véritable Scission dans L'Internationale* begin with the title. 'The Alleged Splits in the International: Private Circular from the General Council of the International Working Men's Association' was written by Marx and Engels in French between January and March 1872, as part of their preparations for the Hague Congress of September 1872 which, among other things, saw the expulsions from the Association of the anarchists Mikhail Bakunin and James Guillaume.[2] First published by Éditions Champ Libre, Paris, in 1972, *The Real Split* was subtitled 'Public Circular of the Situationist International'.

A regular feature of issues 1 to 12 of the Situationist International (SI) journal[3] were the pages given over to news of developments within the SI that the editorial board wished to communicate. For issues 1 and 2 these bore the title 'News of the International' ['Nouvelles de L'Internationale'], for issues 3 to 8 inclusive, that of 'Situationist Information' ['Renseignements situation- nistes'], issue 9: 'The Longest Months (February 1963– July 1964)' ['Les mois les plus longs (février 63–juillet 64)'], issue

10: 'On Some SI Publications' ['Sur des publications de L'IS'], and the lengthier sections in issues 11 and 12 entitled 'The Practice of Theory' ['La Pratique de la théorie']. Issues 11 and 12 also included compilations of the kind of uncomprehending information about, and reactions to, the SI that many organs of the European press were beginning to carry in the years 1967–69. As and when their conferences occurred, reports by the SI of the proceedings were of course also included in the journal.

The seriousness of the crisis into which the world events of 1968 eventually plunged the SI, events that the latter had done so much to foment and whose repercussions are with us to this day, thus prompted Guy Debord as prime mover of the organisation to devote an entire book to the SI and its place in history. Taken together, the experiences of the eighth SI Conference in Venice[4] along with the convoluted and exasperating 'orientation debate',[5] the plain fact that the journal's new editorial team sitting for over a year never came up with 'even 15 lines of usable copy' for a projected issue 13 of the journal, the disturbing emergence of a 'contemplative school' of Situationists within the SI itself and a whole host of 'fans' and 'onlookers' outside it, and thus the very real risk of 'spectacularisation' that the group was now running, seemed indeed to indicate that the organisation in its present form should be wound up. The emergence post-1968 of large-scale movements of anti-capitalist protest and sabotage worldwide was seen as further rationale for the self-dissolution of a separate vanguard of revolutionary extremism which, to all intents and purposes, had accomplished its historical task. If ever the society of the spectacle is to be destroyed, then 'the obscure and difficult path of critical theory must also be the path of the practical movement that occurs at the level of society as a whole'.[6] *The Real Split in the International* is important testimony to the fact that, for a number of years after 1968, proletarian subversion in the industrially advanced countries continued to make itself felt and feared.

*The Real Split* broke new ground in other respects. First, in its brilliant and incisive analysis of the new class relations and conditions in the emerging 'postcolonial', post-industrial society, and in its caustic assessment of the ravages of pollution on the global environment. Withering fire was also trained on the 'pro-situationist disease' (thesis 25 onwards). Few will be unfamiliar with at least some aspects of this phenomenon ever since the 'punk explosion' of the 1970s, all its musical and fashion spin-offs and its innovations in graphic design, not to mention the pro-situ Svengali himself, Malcolm MacLaren.[7] A few years prior to this, at the time of the original publication of *La Véritable Scission*, the attention of people in Britain had been drawn to the long series of outrages and courtroom trials of the mysterious 'Angry Brigade', the rather tenuous pro-situ swagger of whose communiqués also produced their fair share of screaming tabloid headlines.[8]

The last 30 years have seen pro-situ and post-situationist individuals and groups on both sides of the Atlantic devote themselves, often sincerely, to the translation and publication of SI texts and to various publications of their own.[9] Groups like 'King Mob',[10] 'Black Mask', 'The Motherfuckers' were already the subject of polemical debate in the pages of the SI journal itself.[11] Indeed the first English-language translations of the present work were by the American Christopher Winks (1972) and by 'B.M. Piranha', London, UK (1974).[12]

The Real Split in the International is not only essential to an understanding of the revolutionary thought that inspired May 1968 but also an indispensable guide still to all that underpins and is really at stake in the society of the spectacle.

### Notes

1. See appendices 8 and 9.
2. Karl Marx, *Political Writings*, ed. David Fernbach (Harmondsworth, England: Penguin/New Left Review, 1973–4) Vol. 3, *The First International and After*, pp. 272–314.
3. *Internationale situationniste 1958–1969* (ed. Patrick Mosconi, Paris: Arthème Fayard, 1997); partial English translation in Ken Knabb (ed. and trans.), *Situationist International Anthology* (Berkeley: Bureau of Public Secrets, 1981). Website: http://www.bopsecrets.org. Also in Thomas McDonough (ed.), *Guy Debord and the Situationist International* (Cambridge, MA: MIT Press, 2002). See also the multilingual website http://www.geocities.com/debordiana.
4. See appendix 2.
5. *Débat d'orientation de l'ex-Internationale Situationniste* (Centre de Recherche sur la Question Sociale, edited by Joël Cornuault, 80 pp. Paris, 1974).
6. Guy Debord, *La Société du spectacle* (Paris: Gallimard, 1992, coll. Folio 1996) thesis 203; Eng.: *The Society of the Spectacle*, trans. Donald Nicholson-Smith (New York: Zone, 1994). By far the best intellectual biographies to date are those by Anselm Jappe, *Guy Debord* (Marseille: Via Valeriano, 1995; Paris: Denoël, 2001); Eng. trans., Donald Nicholson-Smith with a Foreword by T.J. Clark (Berkeley and Los

Angeles: University of California Press, 1999 – see pp. 99–104 for a critical discussion of *La Véritable Scission*) and by Vincent Kaufmann, *Guy Debord, la révolution au service de la poésie* (Paris: Éditions Fayard, 2001), an extremely penetrating and thought-provoking *tour de force*.

7. One of MacLaren's protégés, John Lydon, has begged to differ however, at least in print: 'All the talk about the French Situationists being associated with punk is bollocks. It's nonsense!... The Situationists ... were too structured for my liking, word games and no work. Plus they were French, so fuck them.' John Lydon with Keith and Kent Zimmerman, *Rotten: No Irish, No Blacks, No Dogs: The Authorized Autobiography of Johnny Rotten of the Sex Pistols* (London: Hodder & Stoughton, 1994).

8. See Tom Vague, *Anarchy in the UK: The Angry Brigade* (Edinburgh and San Francisco: AK Press, 1997).

9. For an extensive list of American and British pro-situ histories publications, individuals, groups and grouplets, see Simon Ford, *The Realisation and Suppression of the Situationist International: An Annotated Bibliography 1972–1992* (Edinburgh and San Francisco: AK Press, 1995). An English-language archive of texts related to the so-called 'Second Situationist International' may be found online at www.infopool.org.uk.

10. See *King Mob Echo: English Section of the Situationist International (Texts 1966–1970)* (London: Dark Star, 2000). Also various fragments in *BAMN (By Any Means Necessary): Outlaw Manifestos and Ephemera 1965–1970*, edited by Peter Stansill and David Zane Mairowitz (Harmondsworth, England: Penguin, 1971; Brooklyn, NY: Autonomedia, 1999).

11. Issue no. 12 of the SI journal, p. 83, 'Les dernières exclusions'; Eng. (excerpts) in Knabb, *Situationist International Anthology, op. cit.*, p. 294.

12. B.M. Piranha, *The Veritable Split in the International*, no copyright, 1974. Revised editions 1985, 1990 under the 'B.M. Chronos' imprint.

# Theses on the Situationist International and its time

One party proves itself to be victorious by breaking up into two parties; for in so doing, it shows that it contains within itself the principle it is attacking, and thus has rid itself of the one-sidedness in which it previously appeared. The interest which was divided between itself and the other party now falls entirely within itself, and the other party is forgotten, because that interest finds within itself the antithesis which occupies its attention. At the same time, however, it has been raised into the higher victorious element in which it exhibits itself in a clarified form. So that the schism that arises in one of the parties and seems to be a misfortune, demonstrates rather that party's good fortune. (Hegel, *Phenomenology of Spirit*)

## 1

The Situationist International imposed itself in a moment of world history as the thought *of the collapse of a world*, a collapse which has now begun before our eyes.

## 2

The Minister of the Interior in France and the federated anarchists of Italy feel the same anger towards it: never had such an extremist project, appearing in an age which seemed to be so hostile to it, taken so little time to assert its hegemony in the struggle of ideas, a product of the history of class struggles. The theory, the style and the example of the SI are adopted today by thousands of revolutionaries in the principal advanced countries; but, on a far deeper level, it is the whole of modern society that seems convinced of the legitimacy of situationist views, whether to realise them or to combat them. Translations and exegeses of SI books and texts are appearing everywhere. Its demands are posted up as much in the factories of Milan as in the University of Coimbra. Its main ideas, from California to Calabria, Scotland to Spain, Belfast to Leningrad, secretly work their way in or are proclaimed in open struggles. Submissive intellectuals who are currently at the beginning of their careers find themselves obliged to adopt the guise of moderate or part-time situationists merely to show that they are capable of understanding the latest stage of the system that employs them. If it is possible for the pervasive influence of the SI to be denounced everywhere, this is because the SI is itself merely the concentrated expression of an historical subversion which is everywhere.

### 3

What are called 'situationist ideas' are merely the initial ideas of the period that is witnessing the reappearance of the modern revolutionary movement. What is radically new about them corresponds exactly to the new characteristics of class society and to the real development of its short-lived triumphs, its contradictions and its repressive means. Everything else is clearly the revolutionary thought engendered over the last two centuries, the thought of history which has returned *perfectly at home* in present-day conditions, not 'revised' on the basis of its own former positions handed down for ideologues to argue over, but *transformed* by contemporary history. The SI's success lay simply in voicing 'the real movement that abolishes the existing state of things', and *in knowing how to voice it*: in other words it was able to begin acquainting the subjectively negative part of the historical process – its 'bad side' – with its own undiscovered[1] theory, one which, despite being initially oblivious to it, this side of social practice creates. The SI itself belonged to this 'bad side'. In the last analysis, it is not therefore a matter of a theory *of the SI*, but of *the theory of the proletariat*.

## 4

Each moment of that historical process of modern society which gives rise to and abolishes the world of the commodity, and which also contains the anti-historical stage of society *constituted as spectacle*, led the SI to be *everything that it could be*. Both in the development of social practice and in the moment which is now emerging as a new era, the SI must increasingly recognise its truth; know what it wanted and what it did, and *how* it did it.

## 5

The SI not only saw modern proletarian subversion coming; it *came along with it*. It did not resort to the icy extrapolation of scientific reasoning in order to announce it as some kind of extraneous phenomenon: rather it went out to encounter it. We did not put our ideas 'into everybody's minds' by the exercise of some outside influence or other, which is something that only the bourgeois or bureaucratic-totalitarian spectacle can do, albeit without lasting success. We gave voice to the ideas *that were necessarily already present* in these proletarian minds, and by so doing we helped to activate these ideas, as well as to make critical action more theoretically aware and more determined to make time its own. Things that are first of all *censored* in people's minds are of course also censored by the spectacle whenever the former have managed to achieve social expression. There is no doubt that this censorship still casts its net over virtually the whole of the revolutionary project as well as over the revolutionary *yearning* in the masses, although theory and critical actions have already made an unforgettable breach in spectacular censorship. The *repressed side* of proletarian critique has emerged; it has acquired a memory and a language. It has undertaken the *judgement of the world* and, with prevailing conditions totally unequipped to plead their cause, the sentence poses only the problem it can solve: that of its execution.

## 6

As had generally been the case in the pre-revolutionary moments of modern times, the SI openly declared its aims and nearly everyone rather fancied it was a joke. The ten-year or so silence observed on this score by social commentators and ideologues of workers' alienation – an extremely short period of time on the scale of such events, but one disrupted in its latter stages by the repercussions of a few scandals quite wrongly held to be incidental and short-lived – had not prepared the false consciousness of grovelling intellectuals to foresee or understand what erupted in France in May 1968, the deepening and extension of which has merely continued up to the present day.[2] That was when the proof furnished by history, and certainly not situationist eloquence, overthrew on this point as on so many others the conditions of ignorance and phoney security maintained by the spectacular organisation of appearances. It is impossible to prove dialectically that one is right other than by appearing in *the moment of dialectical reason*. The occupations movement, just as it drew prompt support in factories in countries the world over, immediately struck society's rulers and their intellectual lackeys as something every bit as incomprehensible as it was terrifying. The property-owning classes, although still trembling before it, understand it better. To the woolly consciousness of the specialists of power, this revolutionary crisis from the word go merely bore the stamp of pure thoughtless negation. The project that it set out and the language that it used were not translatable for these managers of *negationless thought*, a thought hopelessly impoverished by several decades of mechanical monologue, in which inadequacy becomes an end in itself as *ne plus ultra* and in which falsehood has ended up believing in nothing but itself. To whoever rules by the spectacle and in the spectacle, that is, with the practical power of the mode of production which 'has detached itself from itself and established itself in the spectacle as an independent realm', the real movement which has remained outside the spectacle and which came to halt it for the first time, appears as unreality itself in realised form. But what raised such a clamour in France at that moment was merely the self-same revolutionary movement that had begun to make a low-key appearance everywhere else. The first thing that the French branch of the Holy Alliance of society's owners saw in this nightmare was its own imminent demise; next it believed itself saved once and for all; then it ditched both of these errors.[3] For this branch as much as for its partners, *another age* has begun. With it comes the discovery that, as ill-luck would have it, the occupations movement bore a few ideas, situationist ones as it turned out: even people who are unaware of them seem to be using them as the basis upon which to determine their positions. The exploiters reckon on containing them, but despair of ever consigning them to oblivion.

## 7

The occupations movement was the rough sketch of a 'situationist' revolution, but it was no more than a rough sketch both as practice of revolution and as situationist consciousness of history. It was at that moment internationally that a generation began to be situationist.

## 8

The new period is profoundly revolutionary and *it knows it*. At all levels of global society, *people no longer can* nor do they *want* to continue as before. At the top, the peaceful running of everyday affairs is no longer possible because word has got round this sphere that the first fruits of the *supersession of the economy* are not only ripe, but have begun to rot. At the bottom, people are no longer prepared simply to put up with whatever comes their way, and it is the demand *to live* which has at present become a revolutionary agenda. The resolve to make one's history oneself is the secret of all the 'wild' and 'incomprehensible' negations that are holding the old order up to ridicule.

## 9

The world of the commodity, which was already uninhabitable *in essence*, has become so *visibly*. This consciousness is the product of the interaction of two developments. On the one hand, the proletariat wants to possess every aspect of its life, and possess it *as life* in the sense of the totality of its possible realisation. While on the other, at once the dominant science and the science of domination have taken to calculating with pinpoint accuracy the ever-increasing growth of inner contradictions which abolish *the overall conditions of survival* in the society of dispossession.

## 10

The symptoms of the revolutionary crisis are piling up by the thousand, indeed so serious are they that the spectacle is now *compelled to talk about its own ruin*. Its false language evokes its real enemies and the real disaster befalling it.[4]

**11**

The language of power has become wildly reformist. Whereas previously it would show nothing but happiness everywhere in window displays and sold everywhere at the most attractive price, it now slams the ubiquitous failings of its system. Society's owners have suddenly discovered that everything in it must be changed without delay: education as well as town planning, the way work is experienced as well as the horizons for technological development. In short, this world has lost the confidence of all its governments; they therefore propose to dissolve it and set up another one. They wish only to draw our attention to the fact that they are more qualified than revolutionaries to engineer a turnaround requiring so much experience and such considerable means, for possess them they do, and accustomed to them they certainly are. Ready then to dispense largesse come computers with their mission to programme the qualitative, along with pollution *managers* whose self-entrusted paramount task is to lead the struggle against a pollution problem which is of their own making. But modern capitalism already presented itself earlier, in the face of the revolution's past failures, as a reformism *which had succeeded*. It professed to have been the architect of the commodity's particular freedom and happiness. It would one day finish the job of liberating its wage slaves, if not from wage slavery itself, then at least from the copious remains of those extreme hardships and inequalities that its formative period had bequeathed – or, more precisely, from whichever particular hardships capitalism itself judged it should recognise as such. Nowadays it promises to liberate them too from all the new perils and vexations which it is in the very act of producing on a vast scale, as the essential feature of *the most modern* commodity understood in its fullest sense; furthermore, the same fast-expanding production, so highly vaunted up to now as the ultimate corrective for everything, will have to turn itself around while remaining under the exclusive control of the same bosses. The collapse of the old world appears fully in the current ludicrous language of *decomposed domination.*[5]

## 12

Morals improve. The meaning of words plays a part in the improvement. Everywhere *respect for alienation has evaporated.* Youth, workers, people of colour, homosexuals, women and children take it into their heads to want everything that was hitherto *forbidden* them, at the same time as they refuse most of the paltry results that the old organisation of class society *allowed* people to obtain and put up with. They want no more bosses, family or State. They criticise architecture and are learning to talk to one another. Moreover, by rebelling against a hundred specific oppressions, they are in fact taking issue with alienated labour, for what is now clearly on the agenda is *the abolition of wage labour.* Each component of a social space which is more and more directly shaped by alienated production and its planners thus becomes a new arena of struggle, from primary schools to public transport, to mental hospitals to prisons. All the Churches are in decay. Having enjoyed a run for the last 20 years as a mere outlandish comedy act, the curtain is finally coming down, to a collective burst of laughter, on the age-old tragedy of the expropriation of workers' revolutions by the bureaucratic class. Castro has become reformist in Chile, while stage-managing the parody of the Moscow trials at home, after condemning the occupations movement and the Mexican revolt in 1968, yet giving his unqualified approval to the action by the Russian tanks in Prague; the ludicrous double act of Mao Zedong and Lin Piao, at the very same time that this little gang's last faithful Western spectators, whether of the bourgeois or the leftist variety, were finally pointing to the victory it had achieved in the long struggle pitting one exploiter of China[6] against another, lapses back into the terrorist mayhem of that shattered bureaucracy (when the time came, negotiating or refusing to negotiate with the USA was never an issue, but simply ascertaining *who* in Beijing would receive Nixon and his aid, was). If it is possible for humanity joyfully to detach itself like this from its past, it is because *seriousness* and history itself, which reunifies the former in its truth, have both returned to the world stage. No doubt the crisis of the totalitarian bureaucracy, as part of the general crisis of capitalism, is taking on characteristics that are specific to it, as much through the particular social and legal techniques of the appropriation of society by the bureaucracy constituted as a class, as by virtue of its obvious *backwardness* in the development of commodity production. The bureaucracy keeps its place in the crisis of modern society mainly due to the fact that the proletariat is going to destroy it too. The threat of proletarian revolution, which has dominated the entire political agenda of the bourgeoisie and of Stalinism in Italy for the last three years and led to the public alliance of their common interests, is at the same time hanging over the so-called Soviet bureaucracy; to hold the uprising of the workers in Russia in abeyance is *the only real concern* of not only its global strategy (which feared everything from the Czechoslovakian process and nothing from the Romanian bureaucracy's independence), but of its police and psychiatrists too. Already, sailors and dockers all along the Baltic coast have begun again to communicate their experiences and plans to one another. In Poland, with the insurrectional strike of December 1970, workers managed to rattle the bureaucracy and further reduce its economists' room for manoeuvre: price rises were withdrawn, wages were increased, the government fell, and social unrest has remained.[7] But American society is in just as much decay, down to its army in Vietnam, rechristened 'the drug army', who are having to be withdrawn because its soldiers no longer want to fight; and they will fight in the United States. From Sweden to Spain, wildcat strikes are now a Europe-wide feature, with chiefs of industry or their newspapers currently lecturing workers in an attempt to make them see the benefits of trade unionism. In these 'Bacchanalian revels in which no member is not drunk', the British proletarian revolution will not fail this time to keep the appointment: it will be able to drink deep at the wellspring of the civil war which here and now marks the return of *the Irish question*.

In the exploiters, and in many of their victims who have definitively given up on their own lives by neurotically submitting to the reigning order, the decline and fall of this order arouse anxiety and fury. These emotions find primary expression in a fear and a hatred of youth so extreme as to be quite unprecedented. However, at bottom the only fear is that of revolution. Youth, a transient state, represents no threat to the social order; the threat is rather modern revolutionary criticism in actions and in theory, which, from the historic starting point we have just lived through, is growing stronger with each passing year. It may have begun with a particular moment, *but that criticism will not grow old*. The phenomenon is in no way cyclical; it is cumulative. Until recently, youth scared nobody, as long as its rebelliousness appeared to be confined to the student milieu; a milieu, where new-style bureaucratic leftism – which is merely the *kindergarten* of the old world, a play area for people to dress up as a few father-heroes who in fact number among the existing society's founders – actually does its recruiting. Youth became formidable when it was noticed that subversiveness had spread to the majority of young workers, and that the hier-archical ideology of leftism would be unable to co-opt it. This is the youth which is put in prison and which rebels in the prisons. The fact is that youth, while there remains much for it to learn and to invent, and while it still retains, especially among various kinds of professional-revolutionary apprentices, a number of backward traits, has never been *so intelligent*, nor so bent on destroying the established society (the *poetry* which is in *Internationale Situationniste* is now accessible to a young girl of 14 – to that extent Lautréamont's wish has been fulfilled). Those who repress youth want in actual fact to defend themselves against the proletarian subversion with which this youth largely identifies itself, and which they identify with it even more; besides, the very ones making this amalgam sense how lethal it is to them. The panic before youth, which so many inept analyses and pompous sermons seek to hide, is based on a simple calculation: in a mere matter of 12 to 15 years from now, the young will be adult, the adults will be old, and the old people will be dead. The leaders of the class in power desperately need to reverse *their falling rate of control over society* in as few years as possible; and they have every reason to believe that they will not reverse it.

## 14

While the world of the commodity is challenged by proletarians to a degree of intensity never before attained by their criticism, and which is precisely the only one which suited their aims – a critique of the totality – the functioning of the economic system is itself, of its own accord, on course for self-destruction. The crisis of the *economy*, by which we mean the economic phenomenon as a whole, a crisis which has become ever more blatant in recent decades, has just crossed a qualitative threshold. Even the old form of plain *economic crisis* that the system had succeeded in overcoming during the same period, and in the way we know, has resurfaced as a possibility for the near future. This is the result of a dual process. On the one hand, proletarians, not only in Poland but also in England[8] or in Italy, in the form of workers who slip through the net of union control, are laying down demands for higher wages and improved working conditions which are already disrupting the forecasts and decisions of the state economists who oversee the smooth running of concentrated capitalism. The rejection of the present organisation of labour within the factory is already an outright rejection of the society which is based on this organisation, and in this sense some Italian strikes have broken out only a day after the employers had accepted all the previous demands. But the humble wage demand, when it is quite frequently renewed and when, each time, a high enough percentage increase is demanded, clearly shows that workers are becoming aware of their misery and alienation across the *entire spectrum* of their social existence, for which no wage will ever be able to compensate. For example, capitalism having organised workers' urban-fringe housing to its own liking, its occupants will soon be inclined to demand that their mind-numbing hours of daily commuting be *paid* for what they in fact are: an actual *labour time*. In all those struggles which still recognise wage labour, trade unionism must still itself be accepted in principle; however it is only accepted as an apparently ill-suited form which is continually *outflanked*. But trade unions cannot last forever in such social and political circumstances, and *they feel they are wearing out*. In speeches by bourgeois ministers and Stalinist bureaucrats alike, *the same fear* finds the same words to express it: 'I put this question to you: are we going to start all over again like in 1968? To which my answer is: no, it must not start all over again' (statement by Georges Marchais in Strasbourg, 25 February 1972). On the other hand, proletarians of the commodity-abundant society, in the form of consumers who are sick of the tawdry 'semi-durable goods' with which they have long been swamped, are creating some alarming difficulties for the flow of production. So much so that the one avowed aim of the economy's present stage of development, and which is in actual fact the one precondition for everybody's survival in the context of the system based on commodity-labour, viz. *the creation of new jobs*, comes down to the specific task of creating jobs that workers no longer want to take on, in order to produce that increasing share of goods that they no longer want to buy. However, it is at a far deeper level that we need to understand that the commodity economy, with the kind of pinpoint technology whose development is inseparable from its own, *has begun to be racked by death throes*. The recent appearance in the spectacle of a flood of moralizing speeches and pledges of retail solutions to what governments and their mass media call pollution, seeks to hide, at the same time that it must reveal, this obvious fact: capitalism has finally delivered proof *that it cannot develop productive forces any further*. It is not however *quantitatively*, as many people thought it necessary to understand, that capitalism will have proved incapable of pursuing this development, but *qualitatively*. However, quality here is in no way some kind of aesthetic or philosophical demand: it is above all else an historical issue, that of the actual possibilities of the survival of the species. At this moment, Marx's observation that 'the proletariat is revolutionary or it is nothing' finds its ultimate meaning, and the proletariat that has this concrete alternative before it is truly the class that brings about the dissolution of all classes. 'Things have therefore now reached the point where individuals must take possession of the entirety of the productive forces in contention, not only to be able to assert themselves, but once again, in a word, to ensure their existence' (*The German Ideology*).

## 15

The society that has every technical means to modify the biological foundations of the whole of life on earth is also the society that, thanks to the same separate technical and scientific development, has every means of control and of mathematically incontrovertible forecasting to measure in advance exactly what the growth in alienated productive forces of class society can lead to – with dates, according to a best- or worst-case scenario – in terms of the catastrophic break-up of the human environment. Whether it be chemical pollution of the air we breathe or the adulteration of foodstuffs, the irreversible build-up of radioactivity through the industrial use of nuclear energy or the deterioration of water, from underground deposits to the oceans, the town-planning blight whose sprawl is supplanting the former entities of town and country or the 'population explosion', the increase in the number of suicides and the incidence of mental illness[9] or the level of 'noise pollution' – everywhere, *fragmentary* knowledge concerning the (more or less urgent and more or less fatal, as the case may be) impossibility of going any further, tends to form as specialised scientific solutions which remain purely and simply juxtaposed, a portrait of general degradation and *overall impotence*. This woeful summary of the map of the territory of alienation, just prior to its engulfment, is naturally carried out in the same way that the territory itself has been constructed: out of separate sectors. Doubtless this kind of knowledge of the fragmentary will have to take future cognisance, through the unfortunate concordance of all its observations, of the fact that each useful alteration which proves profitable in the short term on a specific point has repercussions on the entirety of the forces at work, and may in time bring about a more decisive ruin. However, such a science, in thrall to the mode of production and to the aporias *of the thought* that this mode has produced, cannot imagine a real overthrow of the present scheme of things. It is quite unable *to think strategically*, not, we might add, that anyone is asking it to do so; besides, it no longer possesses the practical means to intervene in it. Thus all it can talk about is *the expiry date* and the best palliatives that, were they to be strictly applied, would hold this expiry date in abeyance. Consequently what this science demonstrates, to the most ridiculous degree imaginable, is the uselessness of knowledge for its own sake and the nothingness of non-dialectical thought in a period swept along by the movement of historical time. Thus the old slogan, 'revolution or death', is no longer the lyrical expression of rebel consciousness, but the *last word in the scientific thought* of our age. Yet this word can only be spoken by others, and not by that outdated scientific thought *of the commodity* which is revealing the insufficiently rational bases of its development at a time when all its applications are being unfurled in the power of a wholly irrational social practice. It is the thought *of separation*, which has only been able to increase our material sway thanks to the methodological paths of separation, and which ultimately finds this separation realised in the society of the spectacle and in its self-destruction.

## 16

The class that monopolises economic *profit*, having no other aim than that of preserving the dictatorship of the independent economy over society, has so far had to regard and manage the continually escalating productivity of industrial labour as if it were still a matter of *the mode of agrarian production*. It has constantly pursued the maximum amount of purely quantitative production, like those ancient societies which, literally incapable of ever pushing back the limits of genuine want, were compelled each season to harvest *everything that could be harvested*. This identification with the agrarian model finds expression in the pseudo-cyclical model of untrammelled commodity production where not only the objects produced, but also their spectacular images have been intentionally *designed to wear out*, in order to maintain artificially the *seasonal pattern* of consumption, which justifies the continual resumption of productive effort and ensures that penury is always just around the corner. Yet the *cumulative reality* of the production in question, as indifferent to utility or harmfulness as it is in reality indifferent to its own power, *which it wants to ignore*,[10] far from slipping from view, returns in the form of pollution. Pollution is thus a calamity of bourgeois thought; which the totalitarian bureaucracy can only poorly imitate. It is the *ne plus ultra of ideology in material form*, the *wholly contaminated* superabundance of the commodity, as well as the real, miserable dross of spectacular society's illusory splendour.

## 17

Pollution and the proletariat are today the two concrete aspects of the *critique of political economy*. The universal development of the commodity has been wholly confirmed as the crowning achievement of political economy, in other words as the 'abandonment of life'. Once everything entered the sphere of 'economic goods', even such staples as springwater and city air, everything became *economic evil*. The mere sensation of being hemmed in each season by ever more oppressive 'nuisances' and dangers, which have the vast majority of people, that is, the poor, as their immediate and chief point of attack, by now constitutes an immense factor for revolt, a vital demand of the exploited which is every bit as *materialistic* as the struggle waged by workers in the nineteenth century for enough to eat. Cures for the entire range of ailments that production at this stage of its commercial affluence has engendered are already too expensive for it. Relations of production and productive forces have finally reached a point of drastic incompatibility, because the existing social system has cast its lot with the pursuit of a literally intolerable deterioration of all the conditions of life.

## 18

With the new era appears the following admirable coincidence: the revolution is wanted in a total form at a very time when it can only be carried out in a total form, and when the whole functioning of society becomes absurd and impossible without its realisation. The basic fact is no longer so much that abundant material means exist for the construction of free life for a classless society; it is rather that the blind under-use of these means by class society can neither come to a halt nor go any further. Never has such a conjunction existed in the history of the world.

## 19

The greatest productive force is the revolutionary class itself. The greatest development of productive forces currently possible is quite simply the use to which *the class of historical consciousness* can put them, in the production of history as the field of human development, by espousing the practical means of this consciousness: the future revolutionary councils in which the onus will be on all proletarians to decide everything. The requisite definition befitting the *modern* Council – as distinct from its earlier faltering attempts systematically nipped in the bud before they could follow the logic of their own power and thereby experience it – is *the fulfilment of its minimum tasks;* the latter being nothing less than the practical and definitive settlement of *all* the problems that class society is currently incapable of resolving. The sudden collapse of *prehistoric* production, such as can only be brought about by the kind of social revolution we are describing, is precondition enough to usher in a period of great historical production; the indispensable and urgent resumption of the production of man by himself. The sheer scale of the proletarian revolution's current tasks is highlighted in the difficulty it is experiencing in harnessing the primary means for the formulation and communication of its project: to organise itself autonomously and, through this determinate organisation, understand and explicitly formulate the totality of its project in the struggles it is already prosecuting.[11] It is a fact that on this central point, which will be the last to fall, of the spectacular monopoly of social dialogue and social commentary, that the whole world is like Poland: when workers can assemble freely and without intermediaries to discuss their real problems, the State begins to dissolve. Moreover, the strength of the proletarian subversion that has been everywhere on the increase over the last four years can be discerned in the following negative fact: it remains well below the explicit demands that proletarian movements *which never went so far* managed formerly to assert, movements who *thought* they knew their programmes, but who knew them only as *lesser* agendas. The proletariat is in no way disposed to be 'the class of consciousness' through some intellectualist gift or ethical vocation, nor even for the sake of bringing about a realisation of philosophy, but simply because, in the last analysis, it has no other solution than to take possession of history in a period where 'man is at last compelled to face with sober senses, his real conditions of life and his relations with his kind' (*The Communist Manifesto*). What will make workers into *dialecticians* is merely the revolution that this time they are going to have to conduct themselves.

**20**

Richard Gombin, in *The Origins of Modern Leftism*, notes that 'the marginal sects of yesterday have taken on the impetus of a social movement', which has in any case already shown that the revolutionary movement no longer wears the mantle of 'organised Marxism-Leninism'. Thus Gombin legitimately refuses to include the neo-bureaucratic rehashes currently on the market, from the numerous versions of Trotskyism to the varied strands of Maoism, within the ranks of what he very inappropriately terms 'leftism'. Although he appears as charitable as can be towards the few bits of critique hastily spluttered among the submissive intelligentsia of the last 30 years, with regard to the origin of the revolutionary movement, apart from the resurgence of the Pannekoekist tradition of council communism, the Situationist International[12] is basically just about the only thing Gombin can find. Even though 'its enormous ambitions make it worthy of study', present-day subversion is obviously not assured, in Gombin's view, of gaining control of global society. He considers that the opposite could just as well occur, namely the absolute perfecting of 'the era of *management*', so that this subversion would no longer appear historically except as a parting shot in a vain revolt against 'a world which tends towards the rational organisation of every single aspect of life'. Nevertheless, as it is patently obvious everywhere but in the pages of Gombin's book that this world, regardless of its fine intentions and deceitful justifications, has simply gone the way of an unbridled *descent into irrationality* culminating in the present asphyxia, the final alternative formulated by this sociologist has no reality whatsoever. One could hardly, when dealing with such subjects, be more *moderate* than Gombin; and only our unfortunate times could force sociology to embark on such a field study. And yet, through sheer clumsiness, Gombin ends up leaving his readers to ponder no other possible conclusion than a bold pledge about the inevitability of the revolution's victory.

### 21

When all the conditions of social life were changing, the SI, at the heart of this change, could see that the conditions in which it operated transformed faster than all the rest. None of its members could therefore ignore this or contemplate denying it, but in fact many of them *did not want to touch the SI*. It was not even of past situationist activity that they became the custodians, but of its *image*.

### 22

An inevitable part of the historical success of the SI was that it, in turn, began to be *contemplated*, and in such a contemplation the uncompromising criticism of all that exists had come to be *positively appreciated* by an ever-expanding sector of powerlessness itself turned revolutionary. The force of the negative brought into play against the spectacle was *also* slavishly admired by some spectators. The SI's past behaviour had been entirely dominated by the need to act in a period which initially *would not brook any mention of it*. Surrounded by silence, the SI had no support, and many elements of its work were, one by one, continually *co-opted* against it. It needed to reach the stage when it could be judged not 'on the superficially scandalous aspects of certain events providing an arena for it to appear, but on its *essentially scandalous* central truth' (*Internationale Situationniste*, no. 11, October 1967). The calm assertion of *the most sweeping* extremism, like the numerous expulsions of ineffectual or forbearing situationists were the SI's weapons for *this particular* combat, and not in order to become an authority or power. Thus the tone of razor-sharp conceit not infrequently employed in some forms of situationist expression was legitimate; by reason too of the enormity of the task, and above all because it fulfilled its function by enabling the pursuit and eventual success of the latter. However, it ceased to be appropriate the moment the SI came to be acknowledged by a period which no longer regards its project as in any way implausible;[13] it was, moreover, precisely because of the SI's success in this respect that such a tone had become, for us if not for our spectators, *outmoded*. Doubtless the SI's victory may in appearance be as debatable as the one the proletarian movement has already achieved due solely to the fact that the latter has recommenced the class war – the visible part of the crisis which emerges in the spectacle is in no way comparable to its depth – and like that victory too, the SI's will always be *in abeyance* until prehistoric times have reached their end; for anybody, however, who 'can hear the grass grow' this victory is also *unquestionable*. The SI's theory has passed into the masses. It can no longer be liquidated in its original isolation, although it can no doubt still be falsified, albeit in very different conditions. No historical thought can hope to forearm itself against all incomprehension or falsification. Since a definitively coherent and accomplished system is the last thing it claims to supply, then so much less could it hope to appear for what it is in so absolutely rigorous a way that stupidity and bad faith would be forbidden in every one of those who came into contact with it; and in such a way that one true reading of it would be laid down everywhere. The only thing that underpins such an idealistic claim is a dogmatism doomed always to meet with failure, and dogmatism is already the first defeat for such thought. Historical struggles, which correct and improve all theory of this kind, are equally the domain where errors of simplistic interpretation occur such as, very often, self-interested refusals to brook the most unequivocal of meanings. Here, truth can impose itself only by becoming practical force. It shows that it is truth by sole virtue of the fact that inferior practical forces are all that it requires in order to put far greater ones to rout. So much so that if in the future the SI's theory can still be frequently misunderstood or erroneously translated, as has sometimes been the case with those of Marx or Hegel, it will nevertheless be quite capable of reappearing in all its authenticity whenever its time is historically at hand, starting with right now. We have left behind the period in which we could be falsified or dismissed *without appeal*, because from now on our theory benefits, for better or for worse, from the *collaboration* of the masses.

## 23

Now that the revolutionary movement is sole instigator everywhere of serious debate about society, it is *within itself* that it must find the war that it hitherto prosecuted one-sidedly on the outermost edge of social life, appearing at first glance to be completely alien to all the ideas that this society was then able to express concerning what it thought it was. When subversion invades society and spreads its shadow in the spectacle, present-day spectacular forces also emerge within our party – 'a party in the eminently historical sense of the word' – because it has actually had to take on the totality of the existing world, together therefore with all its shortcomings, ignorance and alienations. It falls heir to all the misery, including the intellectual misery, that the old world has produced; for in the final analysis, misery is *its real cause*, although it has had to support such a cause with magnanimity.

## 24

Our party enters the spectacle as an enemy, but as an enemy which is now *known*. The former opposition between critical theory and the apologetic spectacle 'has been raised into the higher victorious element in which it exhibits itself in a clarified form'. Those who, caught up in a tide of fanatical approbation as unadulterated as it is unarmed, *merely contemplate* present-day revolutionary ideas and tasks, devoting particular attention moreover to the SI, furnish overriding proof that at a time when the whole society is compelled to become revolutionary, a vast sector *still cannot.*

### 25

Enthusiastic spectators of the SI have existed since 1960, but in the early years there were only a handful of them. The last five years have seen the handful become a multitude. This process started in France where they were served with the nickname of '*pro-situs*', although this new 'French disease' has now spread to many other countries. Their sheer number does nothing, however, to enhance their vacuity: all of them make it known that they fully approve of the SI, and prove clueless when it comes to doing anything else. By growing in numbers, they remain the same: anybody who has read or seen one has read or seen them all. They are a significant product of modern history but in no sense do they produce it in return. The pro-situ milieu is *in appearance* the SI's theory become ideology – and the passive vogue for such an absolute and absolutely worthless ideology confirms, by manifestly plumbing the depths of absurdity, the obvious fact that the role played by revolutionary ideology came to an end with bourgeois forms of revolution – even though in reality, this milieu expresses that share of authentic modern protest which had to *remain ideological*, imprisoned by spectacular alienation, and *informed* solely of what the latter sees fit to impart. These days, the pressure exerted by history has increased to such an extent that the bearers of an *ideology of historical presence* are forced to remain entirely *absent*.

## 26

The pro-situ milieu possesses nothing but its *good intentions*, and it wants straightaway to consume illusorily their proceeds in the sole form of the terms of its *hollow claims*. Within the SI, the pro-situ phenomenon has come under fire from everybody, in so far as it was seen as a minor, *extraneous* imitation, but then it has not been understood by everybody. It must be regarded not as some superficial and paradoxical mishap, but as the expression of a deep-seated alienation of *the most inactive* part of modern society becoming vaguely revolutionary.[14] We were to experience this alienation as a real *infantile disorder* of the new revolutionary movement as it made its appearance; first because the SI, which can in no way stand apart from, or above, this movement, had been plainly unable to distance itself from this kind of infirmity, and could not hope to avoid the criticism that it demands. On the other hand, were an unfazed SI to continue, in different circumstances, to function as it had done previously, it could well become the revolution's last *spectacular ideology*, as well as the buttress for such an ideology. The SI might then have ended up hampering *the real situationist movement*: the revolution.

## 27

Contemplation of the SI is merely a supplementary alienation of alienated society; but *the mere fact that it is possible* is an upside-down expression of the fact that a real party in the struggle against alienation is currently being formed. Understanding the pro-situs, that is, combating them, instead of merely holding them in abstract contempt on account of their uselessness and the fact that they had no access to the situationist aristocracy, was a basic necessity for the SI. We needed at the same time to understand how the image of this situationist aristocracy came to be formed and exactly which *lower rank* of the SI could smugly exude to the world at large this semblance of increased hierarchical prestige, which only came to it via a *title*: this stratum was itself to be sheer worthlessness gilded with the mere *certificate* of its SI membership. Moreover, not only were such situationists there for all to see, they also demonstrated in practice that their sole desire was to persevere in their *certificated incompetence*. Although defining themselves as hierarchically quite distinct, they held council with the pro-situs in that egalitarian belief according to which the SI could be an ideal monolith where, from the outset, unanimity of thought on each and every subject reigns, and where a perfect outcome likewise rounds off all practical activity: those in the SI who neither thought nor acted were the ones demanding such a mystical status, one moreover to which pro-situ spectators were doing their utmost to draw ever nearer. All who despise pro-situs without understanding them – beginning with pro-situs themselves, each of whom would like to assert his colossal superiority over all the rest – merely hope to persuade others along with themselves that they are saved by some kind of *revolutionary predestination* which would release them from any need to prove their historical effectiveness. Participation in the SI was their Jansenism, just as the revolution is their 'hidden God'. Thus, shielded from historical praxis and believing themselves delivered through some favour or other from the pro-situ's poverty-stricken world, all they could see in this wretchedness was precisely that, instead of also making out the ludicrous part of a far-reaching movement that will ruin the old society.

## 28

What pro-situs saw in the SI was not a specific critical and practical activity explaining or anticipating the social struggles of an era, but simply extremist ideas; and there again, not so much extremist ideas as the idea of extremism; and in the last analysis, less the idea of extremism than the image of extremist heroes gathered together in a triumphant community. In 'the work of the negative', pro-situs dread the negative, and work too. After devoting a rapturous press to the thought of history, their present discomfiture is due to the fact that they understand neither history nor thought. All they need in order to fulfil their dream of asserting an autonomous personality are autonomy, personality and the ability to assert anything whatsoever.

## 29

The overwhelming bulk of pro-situs have learned that there can no longer be revolutionary students, and remain *students in revolutions*. The most ambitious among them feel the need to write, and even to publish their writings so that they can abstractly notify others of their abstract existence, in the belief that they are thereby giving it some substance. However, in this particular field, in order to write, you have to have read, and in order to read, you have to know how to live: this is what the proletariat will have to learn at a stroke in the course of the revolutionary struggle. The pro-situ finds it impossible however to turn a critical gaze on real life since his whole attitude is precisely aimed at illusorily escaping from his pathetic existence by endeavouring to hide it from himself and above all by vainly attempting to mislead everybody else on this score. He must assert that his conduct is *basically* good because it is 'radical', and thus ontologically revolutionary. Compared with this central, wholly imaginary guarantee, he brushes aside umpteen circumstantial errors or comical defects. At best he only recognises these flaws by virtue of the detrimental *result* they have occasioned him. He consoles and excuses himself for them by asserting that he will not commit those errors again and that, on principle, he cannot but be on the path to improvement. Yet he is also powerless in the face of subsequent errors, that is to say in the face of the practical need to understand what he is doing at the very moment of doing it: assessing the conditions, knowing what you want and what to choose, what the possible consequences may be, and how best to handle them. The pro-situ will say that he wants everything because in reality, despairing of ever attaining the slightest actual goal, he wishes merely to inform everybody that he wants everything, in the hope that somebody will then look admiringly upon his confidence and fine nature. He needs a totality which, like him, is devoid of all content. He ignores dialectics because, refusing to see his own life, he refuses to understand *time*. Time scares him because it is made up of qualitative leaps, irreversible choices and once-in-a-lifetime opportunities. The pro-situ disguises time to himself as a mere uniform space through which he will pick his way, going from one mistake to another, one failing to the next, growing constantly richer. Since the pro-situ is always afraid that it applies to him, he hates theoretical criticism whenever it is combined with hard facts, thus whenever it makes its presence felt: every *example* scares him since the only one with which he is overly familiar is his own, the very one he would rather hide away. The pro-situ would like to be original by reasserting what he, at the same time as so many others, has recognised henceforth to be obvious; he has never thought about how he might act in various concrete situations which for their part are original every time. The pro-situ, who sticks to the repetition of a few general remarks, figuring that his errors will thereby lose their specificity and his immediate self-criticisms become milder, lends quite special attention to the problem of organisation because he is seeking the philosopher's stone capable of bringing about the transformation of his warranted solitude into a 'revolutionary organisation' of use *to him*. Since it means absolutely nothing to him, the pro-situ can see the progress of the revolution only in so far as the latter *would have his interests at heart*. So much so that he thinks it advisable on the whole to refer to the 'continued ebbing' of the May 1968 movement. But he is nonetheless most anxious to keep on repeating that the present time is more and more revolutionary, in order to give the impression that the same thing goes for him. Pro-situs raise their impatience and impotence to the level of historical and revolutionary criteria; and in that way they can see virtually no progress being made by anything outside their hermetically sealed hothouse, where nothing in actual fact changes. In the last analysis, every pro-situ is dazzled by the SI's success which, *in their eyes*, adds up without a shadow of a doubt to something spectacular and which they envy bitterly. Obviously every pro-situ who has attempted to sound us out has been given such a rough ride that they are then obliged to reveal, even subjectively, their true colours as *enemies of the SI*, although this still amounts to the same thing since they remain, in the new position they have come to occupy, just as inconsequential. These toothless, ill-tempered runts would very much like to discover *how* the SI managed to function, and even if the SI might not in some way be *guilty* of kindling such a passion; in which case then they would turn the prescription to their advantage. As a *careerist* conscious of his own destitution, the pro-situ is led to put the total success of his ambitions, whose achievement was taken for granted the day he assumed the radical mantle, on immediate display: the dumbest nonentity among them will be found swearing that he has never been more *au fait* than over the last few weeks with good times, theory, communication, the wild life and dialectics; he lacks only a revolution to put the finishing touches to his happiness. He thereupon begins the wait for an admirer who never appears. Attention may be drawn here to the particular form of dishonesty which is revealed in the eloquence gilding this vacuousness. For a start, never does it have more to say about revolution than when it is at its least practical; never does it mouth off the words 'lived' and 'exciting' more than when its language is at its most lifeless and intractable; never does it have the word 'proletariat' on its lips more than when displaying the highest degree of self-importance and swaggering ambition. This really amounts to saying that, in the hands of those wishing to readopt it with no idea how to put it into practice, modern revolutionary theory, having had to fashion a *critique of life as a whole* can only degenerate into a total ideology divesting every single aspect of their wretched lives of *all trace of authenticity*.

## 30

Whereas the SI always knew how to pour unsparing ridicule on the hesitations, weaknesses and miseries of its early endeavours by displaying at each stage the theories, conflicts and rifts that made up its actual history – and especially by placing the complete run of the *Situationist International* journal before the public in 1971, wherein this whole process is chronicled – it is on the contrary *en bloc* that the pro-situs, albeit totally at variance with one another in every other respect, have all constantly claimed to be able to admire the SI. They are careful, however, not to go into universally obvious details of confrontations and choices, so as merely to voice their total approval of the result. Moreover, even though they all have something intrinsically Vaneigemist about them, every pro-situ is currently taking delayed revenge on a floored Vaneigem while overlooking the fact that they have never shown one iota of his former talent; and still they drool over its force, which they understand no better. But the slightest real criticism of what pro-situs are marks their dissolution by explaining the nature of their absence, for they themselves have already continually demonstrated this absence with their attempts to get noticed – all to no avail. As for the situationists who were themselves of a merely contemplative bent – or predominantly so in some cases – and who were wont to arouse a certain interest as members of the SI, their enforced exit from the SI soon brought them face to face with the harshness of a world in which they will be compelled to act *in a personal capacity*; moreover by meeting the same conditions head-on, they nearly all sink back into pro-situ insignificance.

### 31

The real reason why the SI chose early on to stress the collective aspect of its activity and, in relative anonymity, to put its texts before the general public was because without this collective activity, nothing of our project could have been formulated or carried out, and also because we had to prevent the appointment from within our ranks of a few individual celebrities that the spectacle could then have used against our common goal: this succeeded because not one of those who had the means to acquire personal fame, at any rate as long as he or she was a member of the SI, wanted it; and because those who may have wanted it, lacked the means to acquire it. There is no doubt however that in this way the foundations were laid for what subsequently came to pass: the crystallisation of the SI into a *collective star*, the latter an article of blind faith for ardent situphiles. Yet this tactic worked well in the sense that what it enabled us to achieve was vastly more important than the drawbacks it tended to favour at the next stage. When the SI's revolutionary viewpoint was our common project merely *in appearance*, we first of all had to defend the very prospects of it existing and developing at all. Now that it has become the common project of so many people, the needs of the new period are going to rediscover by themselves, beyond the screen of unreal conceptions that cannot be translated into strengths – or even into words – the specific tasks and deeds that the current revolutionary struggle must take on and bear out, and which it will supersede.[15]

## 32

The real, underlying cause of the misery shared by the SI's spectators does not derive from what the SI did or did not do; and the actual influence of a few stylistic or theoretical simplifications of 'situationist primitivism' plays only a very minor part in it. Pro-situs and Vaneigemists are much more the product of the overall weakness and inexperience of the new revolutionary movement, and of the inevitable period of sharp contrast between the magnitude of its task and the limited means at its disposal. The task that anybody takes on who has begun really and truly to endorse the SI is gruelling enough in itself. But in the eyes of mere pro-situs it is absolutely so, whence their immediate rout. Indeed it is the sheer length and roughness of this historical road which creates among the weakest and most pretentious sector of today's pro-revolutionary generation, a generation who, with other words, can still only think and live in accordance with the dominant society's basic norms, the mirage of a kind of *tourist short-cut* towards its infinite goals. As compensation for his real immobility and his *genuine suffering*, the pro-situ consumes the *endless illusion* of being not only *en route* towards it, but literally for ever on the verge of entering the Promised Land of joyful reconciliation with both the world and himself, a place where his insufferable mediocrity will be transfigured into life, into poetry, into something important. This amounts to saying that spectacular consumption of ideological radicality, both in its hope to set itself apart hierarchically from its neighbours and in its permanent disillusionment, is one with the actual consumption of every spectacular commodity,[16] and like it doomed to disappear.

### 33

Those who describe the truly sociological phenomenon of the pro-situs as something unheard-of, something which could not even be imagined prior to the SI's astounding existence, are decidedly naive. Whenever extreme revolutionary ideas have been recognised and taken up by a period in history, a rallying movement, fired in every respect with the same enthusiasm, has ensued among a certain section of youth; particularly among those *déclassé* intellectuals of either the fully fledged or semi-highbrow variety who are striving to occupy a privileged social role, a category whose quantity modern education has vastly increased, but whose quality it has at the same time lowered further still.

Without doubt, pro-situs are more visibly inadequate and wretched because these days the demands of the revolution are more complex and society's ills harder to bear. Nevertheless, the only fundamental difference with those periods when Blanquists, so-called Marxist Social Democrats or Bolsheviks were recruited, lies in the fact that previously these kinds of people were enrolled and employed by a hierarchical organisation, whereas the SI left the pro-situs overwhelmingly on the outside.

## 34

In order to understand pro-situs, an understanding of their social base and *their social intentions* is required. The first workers won over to situationist ideas, workers by and large the products of old school ultra-leftism and thus marked by the scepticism born of long ineffectiveness, were initially very much isolated in their factories and left somewhat blasé by virtue of their still unused, though on occasion quite deep, knowledge of our theories. They nonetheless came to move among, although not without contempt for it, this phoney intellectual pro-situ milieu, with the result that they became imbued with many of its defects. Yet from this point on, most of the workers who have collectively discovered the SI's views, in the wildcat strike or any other form of criticism of their conditions of existence, have in no way become pro-situs. Moreover, these workers aside, those who have undertaken a concrete revolutionary task or who have actually broken with the dominant way of life, are not pro-situs either. The pro-situ can be defined first and foremost by his evasion of such tasks and such a break. Pro-situs are not all students actually pursuing some qualification or other via the examinations sat in these modern-day excuses for universities; nor, with all the more reason therefore, are they all sons of bourgeois. Yet all are linked to a particular social stratum, whether they intend to take genuine possession of its status, or whether they merely wish to consume its specific illusions in advance. This stratum is one of *managers*. Despite the fact that it is certainly most *to the fore* in the social spectacle, it seems to be one with which common or garden leftist thinkers are still unfamiliar, thinkers who have a *vested interest* in sticking to the wholly threadbare résumé of the definition of nineteenth-century class structures: either they wish to conceal the existence of the bureaucratic class in power or aiming for totalitarian power, or else – and more often than not at the same time – they want to conceal their own conditions of existence and their own aspirations as managers clutching petty privileges within the relations of production dominated by the contemporary bourgeoisie.

### 35

Capitalism has continually modified class structure as it transformed social labour in its entirety. It has undermined or reorganised, abolished or even created classes which have a *subordinate* role in the production of the world of the commodity. Only the bourgeoisie and the proletariat – the primordial historical classes of this world – continue between them to play out its destiny in a confrontation which has basically remained the same. But the circumstances, physical surroundings, entourage and even the whole frame of mind of the main protagonists have changed with time, which has brought us to the final act. The proletariat according to Lenin, whose definition in fact corrected that laid down by Marx, was the majority of workers of big industry; the most professionally skilled even being thrust into a suspect position on the sidelines, under the notion of 'worker aristocracy'. Relying on this dogma for support, two successive generations of Stalinists and idiots have continued to dispute whether the workers behind the Paris Commune, workers still fairly close to the craft activity or the workshops of very small industrial concerns, ever were fully fledged proletarians. The same people manage also to puzzle over the existence of the modern proletariat, lost somewhere in a plethora of hierarchical layers, from the 'skilled' assembly-line worker and the immigrant builder to the skilled tradesman and the technician or semi-technician; they even, moreover, make protracted and trivial attempts to establish whether train-drivers personally produce surplus value. Lenin was, however, correct in his estimation that the proletariat *of Russia* between 1890 and 1917 basically only amounted to the workers of modern big industry, which had just emerged over the same period with the recent capitalist development imported into that country. This proletariat aside, the only other *urban* revolutionary force in Russia was the radical part of the intelligentsia, whereas everything had taken quite a different turn in countries where capitalism, with the urban bourgeoisie, had known its natural development together with its original appearance. As with its more moderate counterparts everywhere else, this Russian intelligentsia sought to bring about the political training and supervision of workers. Russian conditions favoured a blatantly political indoctrination in the workplace: the professional unions were dominated by a kind of 'worker aristocracy' who belonged more often to the Menshevik, rather than to the Bolshevik wing of the Social Democratic party, whereas say in England, the equivalent class of trade unionists could remain apolitical and reformist. That the ransacking of the planet by capitalism at its imperialist stage enables it to support a greater number of better-paid, skilled workers, is one observation which, under a moralistic veil, in no way helps us to gauge the revolutionary politics of the proletariat. The latest 'skilled worker' employed in present-day French or German industry, even if he is a particularly ill-treated and destitute immigrant, benefits too from the global exploitation of the jute or copper producer in underdeveloped countries, and is no less of a proletarian for all that. Throughout the history of class struggles, skilled workers with more time, money and education at their disposal have not only supplied smug, law-abiding voters, but just as often furnished extremist revolutionaries as Spartacism and the FAI[*] both serve to show. To regard only supporters and employees of reformist union leaders as a 'labour aristocracy' was in fact to mask the real economic and political issue of the workers' *training and supervision* from without under a controversy shaped by the phoney tenets of economic science. Where the pros-

[*] FAI: *Federación Anarquista Ibérica.* (Publisher's note, Éditions Fayard)

ecution of their vital economic struggle is concerned, workers immediately need to *stick together*. They are beginning to see how *they themselves* can acquire this cohesion in the wider class struggles which, for every one of the contending classes, are at the same time always political ones. But in the daily struggles waged by this class – that is, the very core of their livelihood – which appear to be nothing more than economic and professional ones, the workers first obtained this cohesion through a bureaucratic leadership whose members are at this stage recruited from within this class itself. The bureaucracy is an age-old invention *of the State*. By seizing the State, the bourgeoisie first of all took the state bureaucracy into its service, and only came later on to develop the bureaucratisation of industrial production by *managers,*\* both these forms of bureaucracy being *wholly their own*, and at their entire disposal. It was at a later stage of its reign that the bourgeoisie came to make use *also* of the subordinate and rival bureaucracy which emerged from working-class organisations and even, on the level of global politics and of the maintenance of the existing balance within capitalism's present-day division of labour, of the totalitarian bureaucracy that retains exclusive possession of State and economy in several countries. Once a certain point in the overall development of an advanced capitalist country and its welfare state has been reached, even those classes facing extinction and who, being composed of lone, independent producers, could not invest themselves with a bureaucracy and dispatched only their most gifted

\* In English in the original. (Translator's note)

offspring to posts in the lower echelons of the state bureau-cracy – small farmers, petty bourgeois shopkeepers – place the defence of their interests, in the face of the modern, concentrated economy's sweeping implementation of bureaucracy and state control, in the hands of a few select bureaucracies: 'young farmers' unions, agricultural coop-eratives, or retailers' rights associations. However, the workers at the levers of big industry, those who, Lenin was clearly delighted to learn, had been mechanistically con-ditioned to *military* obedience by factory discipline; to barracks discipline, by means of which he himself intended to make socialism triumph at both party and national level (the kinds of workers who have also dialectically learned the complete opposite), undoubtedly remain if not the pro-letariat in its entirety, then its very core; because theirs is unquestionably the key role in ensuring social production, which they can always bring to a halt, and because they, more than anybody else, are disposed to rebuild it once the abolition of economic alienation presents them with a clean slate on which to do so. All purely *sociological* def-initions of the proletariat, whether conservative or leftist, serve in fact to hide a political choice. The proletariat can only be defined historically, by what it *can* do and by what it can and must want. Similarly, the Marxist definition of the petty bourgeoisie, which has long found such favour as a stupid joke, is also first and foremost a definition based on the position of this class in the historical struggles of its day; but, unlike the definition of the proletariat, it is based on an understanding of the petty bourgeoisie as a wavering and deeply divided class who can only want one contradictory goal after the other, and who do nothing but switch sides according to circumstances. Torn apart in its historical intentions, the petty bourgeoisie has also been, from a sociological point of view, the least definable and well-knit of all the social classes: a craftsman and a university professor, a well-off small shopkeeper and an impoverished doctor, a penniless army officer and a postal worker, the lower clergy and fishing boat skippers could all at one time be lumped together within it. But nowadays, and without of course all these occupations having merged *en bloc* into the industrial proletariat, the petty bourgeoisie of the economically advanced countries has already left the stage of history for the wings where the last defenders of ousted small trade struggle. As a ritual curse that each bureaucrat preaching worker control solemnly hurls at any bureaucrat not active in the same sect as him, it has become nothing more than a museum piece.

### 36

Executives today are the metamorphosis of the urban petty bourgeoisie of independent producers *become wage-earning*. These executives are, for their part too, very diversified, but the actual class of senior executives which functions as the illusory ideal and goal for the others is in fact bound in a multitude of ways to the bourgeoisie, and combines with the latter far more often than it steers an independent course away from it. The bulk of executives consist of middle and junior managers, whose true interests are even less removed from those of the proletariat than those of the petty bourgeoisie were – for the executive never owns the tools of his trade – but whose social concepts and hopes for promotion are firmly tied up with the values and outlook of the modern bourgeoisie. Their economic function is essentially bound up with the tertiary or service sector, and in particular with the strictly spectacular domain of the sale, maintenance and hyping of commodities, including among the latter commodity-labour itself. The image of the lifestyle and the tastes which society specifically manufactures for these, its model offspring, exercises a considerable influence on those groups of poor wage-earners and petty bourgeois longing for career moves into management, and is not without effect on a part of the present-day middle class. The executive is always saying 'on the one hand; on the other' because he knows he has a miserable time of it as a worker but imagines happiness to be his as a consumer. He is a devout believer in consumption for the good reason that he is paid enough to consume a bit more than the others, albeit the same standard commodity: rare are the architects who live in the ramshackle skyscrapers that they put up, but many are the sales assistants behind the counters in fake luxury goods outlets who buy the clothes they are required to distribute onto the market. The typical executive falls between these two extremes; he looks up to the architect, and he is mimicked by the store assistant. The executive is the epitome of the consumer-*spectator*. Constantly insecure and disappointed, the executive is at the centre of modern *false consciousness* and social alienation. Unlike the bourgeois, the worker, the serf or the feudal lord, the executive always feels *out of place*. He constantly longs to be something more than he is and can be. A pretender and a doubter at one and the same time, he is the man of unease, never sure of himself, yet concealing the fact. He is the thoroughly *dependent* man who feels duty bound to lay claim to freedom itself, idealised in his semi-affluent consumption. He is the slave to ambition forever looking to his otherwise miserable future, although he doubts even whether his present post is right for him. It is in no way by chance (cf. *On the Poverty of Student Life*[*]) that the executive is always *the former student*. He is also *the man suffering from withdrawal symptoms*: his drug is the ideology of pure spectacle, the spectacle of *nothing*. It is for his sake, for his work and leisure, that the urban décor is being changed, from office blocks to the tasteless fare dished up in restaurants where he talks loudly to let his neighbours know that he has trained his voice on airport Tannoys. Wanting to be unique and first, he arrives late and *en masse* to everything. In short, according to the revealing new meaning of an old French word of slang provenance, the executive is at the same time *le plouc* [lit. peasant/country bumpkin/yokel, but also fool, twit, clot, idiot, etc. (Translator's note)]. The use of 'man' in the foregoing discussion has of course been motivated by our desire to preserve the simplicity of theoretical language. It goes without saying that the executive is at the same time, and even increasingly, *the woman* who fulfils the same function in the economy and adopts

[*] 'De la misère en milieu étudiant' (Strasbourg: Union des Étudiants de France/Association Fédérative Générale des Étudiants de Strasbourg, 1966); English trans. in print: 'On the Poverty of Student Life', in Knabb, *Situationist International Anthology* (Berkeley: Bureau of Public Secrets, 1981). (Translator's note)

the corresponding lifestyle. Traditional female alienation, which talks about freedom with the logic and intonation of slavery, is intensified by all the extreme alienation of the end of the spectacle. Whether in their work or in their relationships, executives always pretend *to have wanted what they got,* and their secret, agonising dissatisfaction leads them not to want something better, but to have more of the same 'gilded destitution'. Executives being fundamentally separate people, the myth of the happy couple, albeit like everything else contradicted by the sheer weight of evidence readily to hand, enjoys widespread currency in this milieu. The executive basically carries on the sad story of the petty bourgeois because he is poor and would have everyone believe that the rich open their doors to him. The transformation of economic conditions, however, sets them poles apart on several points that are at the forefront of their existence: the petty bourgeois liked to think he was careful with money, whereas the executive must be seen to consume everything. The petty bourgeois was closely associated with traditional values, whereas the executive has to go in pursuit of whatever new gimmick the spectacle happens to churn out from one week to the other. The mind-numbing stupidity of the petty bourgeois was based on religion and the family; the executive's on the other hand fairly melts away into the general flow of spectacular ideology, which never gives him a moment's peace. He may follow fashion to the point of extolling the *image* of the revolution – indeed many were favourable to something of the character taken on by the occupations movement – and these days some of them are even minded to give the situationists their seal of approval.

The behaviour of pro-situs falls entirely within the *structures* of the existence led by executives and primarily, as with the latter, it is theirs far more as an avowed ideal than as a real way of life. Modern revolution, being the party of historical consciousness, finds itself in direct conflict with these proponents and slaves of false consciousness. It must first *drive the latter to despair by making their shame more shameful still!* Pro-situs are in vogue at a time when just about anybody comes out in favour of creating irreversible situations, and when the programme of a ludicrous Western 'socialist' party gallantly sets out to 'change life'. Modesty at any rate has never stopped the pro-situ from notifying everyone that he lives on passions, engages in open dialogue, radically reinvents fun and love, in much the same way that the executive, while at his local wine producer's, comes across the nice little tipple that he will then go off and bottle himself, or stops over at Kathmandu. For pro-situ and executive alike, the present and the future are merely occupied by consumption turned revolutionary: in the immediate sphere, it is above all a question of the revolution of commodities, of the recognition of an endless series of *putsches* by means of which prestige commodities and their demands are replaced; beyond, it is mainly a question of the prestige commodity of revolution itself. Everywhere though lies the same claim to authenticity in a game whose very conditions, made even worse by ineffectual trickery, totally outlaw all trace of authenticity right from the start. Everywhere too is the same spurious quality of dialogue, the same excuse for culture observed hurriedly and from afar. Everywhere the same pseudo-sexual liberation which encounters nothing but the same avoidance of pleasure: on the basis of the same radical, puerile yet thinly veiled ignorance, the never-ending, tragi-comic interplay, for example, between male gullibility and female sham takes root and becomes institutionalised. Yet beyond each and every particular case, *total sham* is their common element. What distinguishes the pro-situ is the way he replaces the flotsam actually consumed by the fully fledged executive with abstract notions. The pro-situ thinks he is able to imitate the mere *sound* of spectacular currency more easily than this currency itself; but he is encouraged in this illusion by the real fact that those com-modities that present-day consumption feigns to admire also make far more noise than enjoyment. The pro-situ will want to possess all the qualities invoked in horoscopes: intelligence and courage, charm and experience, etc., and is surprised, as somebody who has never given a thought to either attaining or using them, that the least practice still comes and upsets his fairytale by this sad stroke of luck *that he has never even been able to simulate them*. In the same way, the executive has never managed to convince any bourgeois, or any executive, that he was above the executive.

## 38

Naturally, the pro-situ cannot disdain the economic goods available to the executive, since the whole of his daily life is governed by the same tastes. He is revolutionary inasmuch as he would like to have them without working;

or rather have them instantly by 'working' in the anti-hierarchical revolution which is going to abolish social classes. Fooled by the easy appropriation [*le détournement*] of the paltry sums allocated in study grants, through which the present-day bourgeoisie in point of fact recruits its junior managerial staff from a variety of social classes – easily writing off that fraction of grant which goes for a while towards the upkeep of future college drop-outs – the pro-situ comes to be secretly of the opinion, even though he himself is unemployed, penniless and talentless, that contemporary society should indeed see to it that he enjoys a fairly comfortable standard of living by sole virtue of the fact that he has proclaimed himself to be an out and out revolutionary because he has declared himself to be one, and an unadulterated one at that. These illusions will quickly evaporate: their duration is limited to the two or three years during which pro-situs are at liberty to think that some economic miracle is going to save them as a privileged elite, although quite how this will happen remains a mystery even to them. Very few will have the stamina and aptitude to wait in this way for the accomplishment of the revolution, which itself would no doubt leave them partly disappointed. They will go to work. Some will be executives and the majority will be badly paid workers. Many of the latter will simply become resigned to their fate. Others will become revolutionary workers.

## 39

At a time when the SI was to criticise some aspects of its own success, which both permitted and obliged it to go further, it found itself to be particularly ill-composed and unfit for self-criticism. Many of its members proved unable even to become personally involved in simply carrying on its earlier activities: they were therefore increasingly tending to form a very high opinion of past achievements, which by this time were beyond their reach, instead of looking to transcend these by setting themselves even more difficult tasks. It had first and foremost been necessary, from 1967 onwards, to set about gaining a foothold in a number of countries where the practical subversion in search of our theory was beginning, and from the autumn of 1968 onwards, we had acted in particular to make the experience and the main conclusions of the occupations movement[17] as well-known abroad as they were in France. This period had seen an increase in members of the SI but not in their quality. From 1970 onwards, autonomous revolutionary elements fortunately resumed, and considerably developed, the most important aspects of this task. Supporters of the SI found themselves, very nearly everywhere that autonomous and extremist working-class struggles were getting under way, in those countries with the most unrest. It was, however, still up to members of the SI to take on the responsibility for the position of the SI itself, and to draw the necessary conclusions from the new period opening up.

## 40

Many members of the SI had never in any way known the time when we observed that 'strange emissaries are travelling through Europe and beyond; bearers of incredible

instructions are known to meet' (*SI*, no. 5, December 1960).
Now that such instructions are no longer incredible but
become more complex and more sharply focused, these
comrades failed in nearly every circumstance where they
needed to formulate or endorse them; and several even
preferred not to go that far. Beside those who had in fact
never actually joined the SI, two or three others who had
displayed some merit in poorer but calmer years, though
positively worn out by the actual advent of the era they
had been hoping for, had in fact left the SI, but without
wanting to admit it. It then had to be acknowledged that
several situationists could not even grasp what putting
new ideas into practice might involve, nor for that matter
the reverse procedure of rewriting theories with the help of
facts; and yet this was precisely what the SI had achieved.

### 41

The fact that the first situationists knew how to think,
take risks and live, or that among the many to have disap-
peared, several ended up committing suicide or in mental
institutions, could in no way *hereditarily* confer courage,
originality or a sense of adventure on each of the latest
arrivals. The more or less Vaneigemist idyll – motto: *Et in
Arcadia situ ego* – cloaked the lives of those who gave no
proof of their quality either in their contribution to the SI
or in anything to do with their personal existence in a kind
of legal form of abstract equality. By resuming this *still
bourgeois* conception of revolution, they were merely
*citizens of the SI*. In every circumstance of their lives, they
were in actual fact men *of approbation*; being in the SI,

they fancied salvation to be theirs by placing everything under the fair sign of historical negation, even though all they gave this negation itself was their muted approval. Those who never used the words 'I' and 'you', but always 'we' and 'one', were often not even par for the course of political activism, whereas the SI had from the outset been a project much vaster and deeper than a simply political revolutionary movement. Two miracles coincided which to them seemed due by the nature of creation to their own discreet yet profound lifelessness: the SI spoke, and history confirmed it. The SI had to be all things to those members who did nothing, and who, even elsewhere, did not amount to much. Thus widely differing and even conflicting weaknesses tended to bear each other up within the contemplative unity founded upon the SI's excellence; an SI that was supposed, moreover, to guarantee the excellence of what was all too plainly mediocre in the rest of these members' existence.[18] The dreariest ones talked about fun, while the most resigned talked about passion. Membership of the SI, even in its contemplative form, was to be proof enough of all this, with which nobody otherwise would have dreamt of crediting them. Although numerous observers, policemen or others, denouncing the direct presence of the SI in umpteen rebellious activities that are developing very well along their own lines right across the world, may have given people the impression that every member of the SI was working 20 hours a day to revolutionise the planet, we should stress here the falseness of this image. History will, on the contrary, show the considerable *economy of forces* by means of which the SI managed to do what it did. So that when we say that some situationists were doing really too little, this should be taken to mean that they were literally doing next to nothing. We would add the following notable fact here which very much confirms the dialectical existence of the SI: there was no kind of opposition between theorists and practitioners of revolution, or of anything else for that matter. The best theorists among us have always been the best in practice, and those who cut the sorriest figures as theorists were also the most helpless before any kind of practical question.

**42**

The contemplatives in the SI were pro-situs *perfected*, for they saw their imaginary activity endorsed by the SI and by history. The analysis we have carried out of the pro-situ and his *social position* fully applies to them, and for the same reasons: the ideology of the SI is borne by all who were themselves incapable of managing the SI's theory and practice. The '*Garnautins*' expelled in 1967 had been the first instance of the pro-situ phenomenon in the SI itself, although it had thereafter continued to spread. For the green-eyed angst racking the common pro-situ, our contemplatives substituted an appearance of quiet enjoyment. Yet their own non-existence, coming into conflict with the demands of historical activity which are in the SI – not only in its past but now present in ever larger numbers with the expansion of modern-day struggles – caused their anxious dissimulation and led them to be even more ill at ease than the pro-situs on the outside. The hierarchical relationship that existed in the SI was of a new type, one *turned on its head*: those subjected to it concealed it. In fear and trembling before the very real prospect of it collapsing any minute, they hoped with mock bemusement and sham innocence to spin it out for as long as possible, for some of them fancied too that it would soon be time to pick up a few historical rewards; and never did they receive them.

## 43

We were there to combat the spectacle, not govern it. The craftiest ones among the contemplatives no doubt believed that everybody's commitment to the SI would call for solicitous treatment of their numbers or, in one or two cases, their reputation. Nevertheless in this, as in everything else, they were mistaken. This 'party loyalty' lacks any kind of foundation in the context of the SI's genuine revolutionary action – 'The situationists do not constitute a separate party. ... Their interests are no different from those of the proletariat as a whole' (*Avviso al proletariato italiano sulle possibilità presenti della rivoluzione sociale*, 19 November 1969) – and the SI has never been something to be treated with kid gloves;[19] and even less so at the present time. In an extremely harsh age, the situationists willingly chose a particularly tough set of rules; and have for the most part abided by them. We needed therefore to drive out these useless elements who could speak only to lie about what they were, and repeat glorious promises about what they could never be.

## 44

If the SI came to be contemplated as revolutionary organisation *per se*, existing in ghostly fashion as the pure idea of organisation, and becoming for many of its members an outside entity distinct both from what the SI had actually achieved and from their personal non-achievement, yet haughtily covering up these contradictory realities, it was obviously because such contemplatives had not understood, nor wished to know, what a revolutionary organisation could be, and not even what *theirs* had managed to be. This lack of understanding is itself produced by the inability to think and act in history, and by individual defeatism which shamefully recognises such an inability and, far from wanting to overcome it, seeks rather to conceal it. Those who, instead of asserting and developing their real personalities in critical and decision-making activities which bore on what the organisation was doing and could do at any moment, chose to sit back and systematically rubber-stamp decisions already taken, were in fact just out to hide this whole play of appearances by their imaginary identification with the result.

## 45

Ignorance about organisation is the central ignorance about praxis; and whenever it is *deliberate* ignorance, it merely denotes the fearful intention to remain outside historical struggle, while pretending, for Sundays and holiday occasions, to go strolling alongside it like well-informed and demanding spectators. Error about organisation is the *central practical error*. If it is intentional, it aims to use the masses. If not, it is at least total error about the conditions of historical praxis. It is therefore fundamental error in the very theory of revolution.

### 46

The theory of revolution in no way falls exclusively within the domain of strictly scientific knowledge, and even less within the construct of a speculative undertaking or the aesthetic quality of the kind of inflammatory talk that gazes at itself in its own lyrical glow and finds that it is already warmer. Only with its practical victory does this theory exist in any real sense: here, 'great thoughts must be followed by great deeds; they have to be like sunlight, which produces what it shines upon'. Revolutionary theory is the domain of danger, the domain of uncertainty; it is forbidden to people who crave the sleep-inducing certainties of ideology, including even the official certainty of being the strict enemies of all ideology. The revolution in question is a form of human relations. It is part of social existence. It is a conflict between general interests concerning social practice as a whole, and only in this respect does it differ from other conflicts. The rules of conflict are its rules, war is its means, and its operations are more comparable to an art than to a piece of scientific research or a catalogue of good intentions. The theory of revolution is judged on the sole criterion that its *knowledge* must become a *power*.

The revolutionary organisation of the proletarian period is defined by the different moments of the struggle, where each time the onus is on it to succeed; the onus is also on it, in each and every one of these moments, to succeed in not becoming a *separate power*. No discussion of it can be viable that chooses to ignore either the forces it brings into play in the here and now, or the corresponding actions of its enemies. Each time it manages to take action, it unites the theory and the practice that constantly proceed from one another, although never for one moment does it believe it can achieve this through some gratuitous demand for their total merger. When the revolution is still a long way off, the difficult task for revolutionary organisation is above all *the practice of theory*. When the revolution commences, its difficult task comes down increasingly to *the theory of practice*; although the revolutionary organisation has by then assumed a completely different form. In the former case, few individuals are *ahead of their time* [*d'avant-garde*], and they must prove they are by the coherence of their overall project and by the practice which enables them both to experience and communicate it; in the latter, the masses of workers are *of their time* and must remain there as its sole possessors by mastering the use of all their theoretical and practical weapons, and particularly by refusing all delegation of power to a separate vanguard [*avant-garde*]. Again, in the former case, around ten effective men are enough to usher in the self-explanation of an era containing a revolution it is still unaware of and which seems to it everywhere to be absent and impossible:

in the latter, the great majority of the proletarian class must hold and exercise all powers by organising themselves into permanent deliberative and executive assemblies which nowhere allow any manifestation of the old world and of the forces that defend it to survive.

## 48

Wherever they organise themselves as the actual form of society in the throes of revolution, proletarian assemblies are egalitarian, not because every individual is involved in them to the same degree of historical intelligence, but because *together these individuals literally have everything to do*, and because jointly they possess every means of doing it. The overall strategy of each moment is their direct experience: they have to employ all their forces within it as well as immediately brave all its risks. Both in the triumphs and the failures of the concrete collective undertaking in which they have been compelled to bring their entire lives into play, historical intelligence reveals itself to each and every one of them.

## 49

The SI never presented itself as a model of revolutionary organisation, but as a specific organisation that devoted itself in a particular period to specific tasks, and even in this regard it never managed to articulate everything it was, nor managed to be everything it articulated. The organisational errors committed by the SI *in its own concrete tasks* were caused by the objective inadequacies of the previous period, and also by the subjective inadequacies in our understanding of the tasks of such a period, of the limits we encountered, and of the *compensations* many individuals create for themselves as a cross between what they would like to do and what they can do. The SI, which understood history better than anybody else in an anti-historical period, nevertheless still *had too little understanding of history*.

## 50

The SI was always anti-hierarchical, but hardly ever managed to be egalitarian. It was right to support an organisational agenda with a strong anti-hierarchical bias, and to act constantly itself in accordance with strictly egalitarian rules, through which all its members were acknowledged to have an equal right to decision-making, and were even in a tremendous hurry to use this right in practice. But the SI was very wrong indeed not *to catch better sight*, and not *to give more accurate report* of the partly inevitable, partly circumstantial obstacles that it encountered in this area.

## 51

The danger of hierarchy, which is necessarily present in any genuine avant-garde, has its real historical measure in an organisation's relationship with the outside world and with the individuals or masses that this organisation can control or manipulate. On this point the SI managed never in any way to become a power: a result obtained not only by shutting out hundreds of its self-confessed or potential supporters, but also by very often forcing them to embrace autonomy. The SI, as we know, only wished to allow a tiny number of people to become members. History has shown that this was not enough to guarantee, at the stage of such an advanced undertaking, 'participation in its total democracy ... the recognition and self-appropriation by all ... of the *coherence of its critique* ... both in the critical theory proper and in the relationship between this theory and practical activity' ('Minimum definition of revolutionary organisations', adopted by the seventh Conference of the SI, July 1966). But this limitation was to be of much more use in safeguarding the SI against the different possibilities of *command* that a revolutionary organisation, *whenever it succeeds*, can bring to bear in the outside world. Thus it is not so much that the SI is anti-hierarchical that it had to restrict itself to a tiny number of supposedly equal individuals, but much rather because the SI never wanted to throw anything but this tiny number into its activity that it proved to be truly anti-hierarchical in the key areas of its strategy.

## 52

As for the inequality which was so often displayed in the SI, and never more so than when it brought about the recent purge in its membership, on the one hand it has a familiar anecdotal ring to it, since the very situationists actually accepting a hierarchical position turned out to be precisely the weakest ones: by discovering their worthlessness in practice, we fought once more against the triumphalist myth of the SI, and confirmed its truth. On the other hand, a lesson should be drawn from the foregoing which generally applies to all periods of avant-garde activity – from which we are only just emerging – periods in which revolutionaries find themselves compelled, even though they may prefer to ignore it, to play with the fire of hierarchy and do not all turn out to be blessed, as the SI was, with the ability to emerge unscathed: *historical theory is not the locus of equality*, the periods of egalitarian community are its blank pages.

### 53

From now on, situationists are everywhere, and so is their task. All who think it theirs have simply to prove 'the truth, which is to say the reality and the power, the materiality' of their thought before the whole of the revolutionary proletarian movement wherever it is beginning to create its International, and no longer merely before the SI. For our own part, we no longer have to give any kind of *assurance* whatsoever that such and such an individual is or is not a situationist; and not only because we *no longer need to*, but because we have never wanted to. But history is an even harsher judge than the SI. We can on the other hand guarantee that those who were forced to leave the SI without finding what they had long assured everybody they had found – the revolutionary realisation of themselves – and who therefore quite naturally found nothing more than a stick with which to beat themselves, are no longer situationists. The very term 'situationist' was only used by us in order to *pass on*, with the resumption of the social war, a certain number of views and theses: now that this is done, this situationist label, in an age that still needs labels, may well be for the revolution of a whole era to keep, albeit in a totally different way. Furthermore, how a certain number of situationists may be led to associate directly with one another – and first for the current, specific task of moving from the initial period of new revolutionary slogans adopted by the masses to the historical grasp of theory in its entirety, and to its necessary development – will be up to the course of practical struggle, and not some set of organisational assumptions, to determine.

## 54

The first revolutionaries who wrote intelligently about the recent crisis in the SI, and who achieved the best understanding of its historical meaning, have so far neglected a crucial dimension to the practical side of the whole issue: because of everything it has done, the SI actually holds a certain practical power, which it has only ever used in self-defence, but which clearly could, by falling into the wrong hands, have had disastrous consequences for our project. Applying to the SI the criticism it had so precisely applied to the old world is not simply a theoretical affair either, in a field where our theory moreover encountered no opposition: it was a specific critical and practical activity we undertook in *breaking up* the SI. A handful of *arrivistes*, for example, securing the routine loyalty of a few honest comrades whose very weakness inclined them to be undemanding and lacking in foresight, could well have attempted to keep control of the SI for a while, at least as an object with a certain *negotiable prestige*. For those who in every other respect were so defenceless and so unimportant, this was the only weapon and the only importance they had. Only the awareness of their own undue incompetence kept them from actually using such a weapon; although they just may have felt compelled in the end not to use it.

**55**

The orientation debate of 1970, along with the practical questions that needed to be settled at the same time, had shown that the SI's criticism which met with everybody's instant approval in principle, could only become true criticism by going as far as a practical breach, for the absolute contradiction between agreements ratified over and over again, and the paralysis in practical matters with which many were stricken – including the slightest practice of theory – formed the very heart of this criticism. Never in the history of the SI had a split been so predictable and therefore in urgent need of execution. Throughout the course of this debate, those who made up the then-existing majority of SI members – and a shapeless, disunited, passive majority at that, devoid moreover of any proper viewpoint – had been given an extremely rough ride by a tiny minority, and quite rightly so. It had in all honesty become impossible to show further consideration for these people. And it is well known that 'men must be either pampered or crushed, because they can get revenge for small injuries but not for grievous ones'.

## 56

A declaration was then enough that a split had become necessary. Each one had to choose sides; and each one moreover got their chance, since the question to be settled ran infinitely deeper than the blatant shortcomings of such and such a comrade. The fact that this enforced split has failed to produce one single secessionist *on the other side* capable of standing up for himself, in no way alters its nature of a real split but bears out the actual content of it. As the numbers in the SI decreased, the manoeuvring skills of all the members who might have wished to keep something of the *status quo* dwindled. The very fact that this split was designed to put a stop to the easy time once had by the 'situationists' whose declarations and countersignatures went no further than the paper they were written on, made it increasingly impossible for others to carry on in the same vein of bluff without the appropriate conclusions being immediately drawn. Those without the means to fight for what they want or against what they do not, can only expect to stay around for so long.

## 57

Unlike the earlier purges which in less favourable historical circumstances had to aim at reinforcing the SI, and did reinforce it each time, this one aimed at *weakening it*. There is no such thing as a supreme saviour: it fell to us once again to prove it. The method and the aims of this purge were of course approved by every single one of the revolutionary elements on the outside with whom we were in contact. It will be readily appreciated that what the SI has done over the recent period while observing a relative silence, and for which the present theses seek to provide an explanation, constitutes one of its most important contributions to the revolutionary movement. Never have we once been involved in anything either politicians of the most extreme left-wing variety or the most progressive-minded intellectuals get up to in the way of business, rivalries and the company they keep. Now that we can moreover pride ourselves on having achieved the most revolting fame among this rabble, we fully intend to become *even more inaccessible*, even more clandestine. The more famous our theses become, the more shadowy our own presence will be.

### 58

The real split in the SI was the very one which must now take place in the vast and formless protest movement currently at work: the split between, on the one hand, all the revolutionary reality of the present age, and on the other, all the illusions about it.

### 59

Far from claiming to hold others fully responsible for the SI's defects, or to explain them by means of the psychological peculiarities of a few hapless situationists, we on the contrary accept these defects as having also been part of the historical operation that the SI carried out. The game was not somewhere else. Whoever created the SI, whoever created the situationists, must have created their faults as well. Whoever helps the present age to discover its potential is no more shielded from this age's defects than free from what could happen to produce total disaster. We recognise the entire reality of the SI and, on the whole, are delighted that it should be so.

## 60

May we cease to be admired as if we could be superior to our times; and may the present age terrify itself in self-admiration *for what it is.*

## 61

Whoever considers the life of the SI will find therein the history of the revolution. Nothing has been able to sour it.

Guy Debord, Gianfranco Sanguinetti[*]

### Notes

1. 'Chotard! Now do you see you're a fool and a political dwarf? ... Will you ever understand that there is no theory and practice other than that of the proletariat itself; that a theory is situationist only to the extent that situationists themselves lay bare the stages and details of it? ... Opposition to the "concepts" of others is the only course left to all who think that theory is an assemblage of concepts, principally their

---

[*] This latter signature was included by Guy Debord as a tribute to Gianfranco Sanguinetti, who had been expelled from France on 21 July 1971 by Interior Ministry decree. (Publisher's note, Éditions Fayard)

own. Were the propaganda and lies they espouse actually to subjugate the masses, they would still be wondering how such an event could possibly have occurred. They would never know the architect of this success nor even what its ingredients were. ... Nobody will be surprised at the idea of the proletariat realising theory if for the proletariat this means transforming the world as well as knowledge. It will doubtless come as no surprise even to Chotard. What scares him though is that the proletariat might realise situationist theory and not his' (Juvénal Quillet and Schumacher, *History of the Council of Nantes*, Nantes 1970).

2. 'Writing about situationist theory at the beginning of 1968, a critic referred mockingly to "a little glimmer that ambles from Copenhagen to New York". I'm afraid that the very same year the "little glimmer" turned into a sudden conflagration which ripped through every citadel of the old world. ... The situationists brought the theory of the underground movement which permeates modern times to the surface. While Marxism's bogus heirs were overlooking the share of the negative in a world so chock-full of positivity, and were at the same time dropping dialectics off at the antique dealer, the situationists not only announced the resurgence of this self-same negative but could also discern the reality which underpinned these self-same dialectics whose language and "insurrectional style" (Debord) they rediscovered' (François Bott, 'The situationists and the cannibal economy', *Les Temps modernes*, nos 299–300, June 1971).

3. 'A new awareness (as well as a new take on language) which has its source in the intellectual (and practical) activities of a minority of insolent yet lucid anti-establishment figures: the Situationist International. Now for over ten years, by an apparent paradox whose secret lies with history, the SI has remained virtually unknown in our country. All of which could lend justification to the following reflection by Hegel: "Every important, instantly recognisable revolution must be preceded in the *Zeitgeist* by a secret revolution which it is not given to everybody to see. It is moreover even less of an

observable phenomenon for contemporaries, and is as difficult to express in words as it is to understand"' (Pierre Hahn, 'The Situationists', *Le Nouveau Planète*, no. 22, May 1971).

4. 'Ever since its publication in 1967, *The Society of the Spectacle* ... has been fuelling debates within every far-left political circle. Some consider this work, which predicted May 1968, to be the *Das Kapital* of the new generation' (*Le Nouvel Observateur*, 8 November 1971).

5. 'The thing which strikes me in present-day advertising is the extent to which the language it uses is outmoded. Its origins go back to before the great fissure that, albeit largely hidden by life's hard knocks, has been cutting a zig-zag through society ever since 1968. ... Advertising will have to integrate the problems of civilisation into its scheme of things if it wants to be really profitable; in other words it cannot confine itself to selling in the short-term; its medium and long-range goals must treat the consumer to high doses of the "feel-good factor". ... Motivational surveys – which I have been responsible for piloting in France – have provided us with the keys to a thorough understanding of the consumer; but generally speaking they are used only to forge a vernacular that remains one-way. Tomorrow's advertising will have to go down the road of real communication, where both speakers come under and take account of each other's influence, in a dialogue conducted as far as possible on equal terms' (Marcel Bleustein-Blanchet, *Le Monde*, 9 December 1971).

6. 'The *Warlords* are already reappearing in the uniforms of independent "Communist" generals, dealing directly with the central power and following their own policies, particularly in the outlying areas. ... It is the worldwide break-up of the *Bureaucratic International* which is now re-occurring at the Chinese level in the fragmentation of the régime into independent provinces. ... The *proletarian "Mandate of Heaven"* has expired' (*Internationale Situationniste*, no. 11, October 1967).

7. 'Comrades, a word in your ear. I hope that a new start really is what comrade Gierek is talking about in his speeches to

us. If this is the case, then he should get our support. How? Through dialogue, since the only weapon we have is plain speaking. Lies are of no use to us. We must ensure that the discussions continue along these lines. The workers are well aware that our ruling classes are now home to two trends which are at total variance with one another. If the one that was the driving force behind the old policies regains ground, then as former strikers we will all be locked up. I would like to reply to comrade Gierek when he says that we must save money and that money is a precious thing where we live. Don't we know it. Our very own blood is part and parcel of it. But we can always extract money from those who live too well. To put it bluntly comrades: our society is dividing into classes' (Speeches by two branch delegates from the 'A. Warski' shipyards in Szczecin, 24 January 1971, published in *Gierek face aux grévistes de Szczecin*, Éditions SELIO, Paris, 1971).

8. 'It is plain to see that the miners have won a near total victory. ... Acting only just within the law, the strikers managed to halt deliveries of the coal already brought to the surface, along with deliveries of the alternative fuels bound for the power stations. ... The wage rises awarded range from 15 to 31% and are therefore far in excess of the 8% cap that the government had succeeded in placing on public and private sector wage demands. ... In short, the settlement should not act as a precedent for other groups of workers to take advantage of. The government is all the same hoping in this way to salvage its wages policy, although seasoned commentators on economic affairs are sceptical about Mr. Heath's chances of holding out now against the railway workers, bus drivers, teachers and nurses, whose wage claims are in the region of 15 to 20%, if not on occasion higher' (*Le Monde*, 20–21 February 1972).

9. 'According to the annual figures for the population of France as a whole, over the last 20 years (1950–70) the incidence of chronic illness due to mental breakdown has quadrupled; at the present time, according to figures for the Paris region,

these ailments account for a quarter (24%) of all authorised leave. ... Such an increase, similar to that registered in every other so-called industrialised country, obviously cannot be the result of some hereditary degeneration or other running like wildfire through their citizenry. Neither is it due, as is the case in other branches of pathology, to a marked advance in the techniques used to screen for mental illness. ... The role of psychiatrists is to prevent or to treat mental disturbances, and not to seek somehow or other to cure these mass neuroses from the moment it becomes clear that the sheer number of them is not an indication of turmoil on an individual level so much as the way social structures are ill-adapted to most people's emotional frame of mind' (Dr Escoffier-Lambiotte, *Le Monde*, 9 February 1972).

10. 'The economy's triumph as an independent power inevitably also spells its doom, for it has unleashed forces that must eventually destroy the *economic necessity* that was the unchanging basis of earlier societies. ... Such an autonomous economy irrevocably breaks all ties with authentic needs to the precise degree that it emerges from a *social unconscious* that was dependent on it without knowing it. ... By the time society discovers that it is contingent on the economy, the economy has in point of fact become contingent on society. Having grown as a subterranean force until it could emerge sovereign, the economy proceeds to lose its power' (*The Society of the Spectacle*).

11. 'Such a theory expects no miracles from the working class. It views the reformulation and satisfaction of proletarian demands as a long-term undertaking' (*The Society of the Spectacle*).

12. 'But they do not claim to have made the only correct exegesis of Marx: in fact they go beyond Marx, and are not Marxists in the modern sense. ... It will be seen that there is something radical in this conception; the break it entails with the whole left movement of this half-century endows it with a somewhat millenarian, heretical hue. ... By the middle of the 1960s, if not earlier, the situationists foresaw and

predicted "the second proletarian assault against class society". ... The style they have developed and which has reached a remarkably high level of cohesion has adopted some of the techniques of Hegel and the young Marx, such as the reversed genitive (the weapons of criticism, the criticism of weapons), dadaism (a rapid flood of words, words used in senses different to their conventional meaning, etc.). But above all, it is a style permeated by irony. ... On the eve of the "events of May" 1968, the situationists believed that the historic hour was at hand. ... In the course of the 'événements' of May–June 1968, the situationists had the opportunity of applying their ideas, both on fundamental issues and on the question of organisation, initially in the first occupation committee of the Sorbonne, and subsequently in the committee for maintaining the occupations (CMDO: *Comité pour le Maintien des Occupations*)' (Richard Gombin, *Les Origines du Gauchisme*, Éditions du Seuil, Paris 1971; Eng. trans. by Michael K. Perl, *The Origins of Modern Leftism*, Harmondsworth, Middlesex: Penguin Books, 1975).

13. 'When one reads or rereads back issues of the SI journal, it is indeed striking to note just to what extent and how often these *maniacs* have passed judgments or set forth points of view that were subsequently borne out in reality' (Claude Roy, 'Les Desesperados de l'espoir', *Le Nouvel Observateur*, 8 February 1971).

14. 'Pro-situ regression was regarded alternatively as a quirk, as the dregs of a movement, as a trendy fad, but never for what it was in reality: the qualitative weakness of *the whole*, a necessary moment in the overall progress of the revolutionary project. *Situationism* is the adolescent crisis of a situationist practice which has reached a decisive point in the initial crucial stage of its growth, a point where it must master in practice the spectacle that is gaining hold of it. ... It is this comfortable settling down into a positive furrow that characterises the *situ role*; indeed, the more *de facto* the objective place occupied by the SI in present-day history

became (and the same will go for all future revolutionary organisations), the more hazardous its legacy became for each one of its members to assume. ... May 1968 was the realisation of modern revolutionary theory, its overwhelming confirmation, just as it was to a certain extent the realisation of the individuals who participated in the SI, notably in the revolutionary lucidity they evinced within the movement itself. For the SI, however, the occupations movement *remained the conclusion* of its long practical researches, without for all that denoting their transcendence. ... While the situationists were calling their own existence into question on a practical level by embarking on an "orientation debate" in an effort to determine the forms best suited to the next stages of their development, the satellite groups they had given rise to lagged way behind, taking the SI as a pristine model and organising themselves exclusively on the flimsy basis of a limited implementation of the odd assurance here and there, the latter derived from the SI's experience in times gone by' (*To Clarify Some Aspects of the Here and Now* [anonymous pamphlet], Paris, January 1972).

15. 'The real strength of situationist theory lies in its ability to infiltrate, like heavy water. *Let's go on,* but don't let's leave it at that. Moreover, the question of non-dialectical supersession is being posed again. Politics has not come up with any answer. The area is a sensitive one, and politics tends merely to protract the issue. We need then to start again from scratch and it is in this respect that I am a situationist in 1971. As for what it means to be in the International! Resumption of the undermining work pioneered by the situs of '57 is the task. This is what remains of the SI. ... The SI is right, an era, by now perhaps the twentieth century itself, has passed, and the fact that "nobody has thus far taken more effective steps towards leaving the twentieth century than it has" (*SI*, issue no. 9) has been driven home. I'm convinced that the practical and theoretical distance which was ushered in over the last ten years between the First International and the Situationist International is the very one which now remains to be estab-

lished between the Situationist International and what we need to do. Is this not something that the SI is aware of too?' (Bartholomé Béhouir, *De la conciergerie internationale des situationnistes*, Paris, August 1971).

16. 'The image of the blissful unification of society through consumption suspends disbelief with regard to the reality of division only until the next disillusionment occurs in the sphere of actual consumption' (*The Society of the Spectacle*).

17. 'The observer can only be struck by the speed with which the contagion ripped through the entire university as well as through a large swathe of non-university youth. It seems then that the slogans issued by the tiny minority of genuine revolutionaries stirred up something indefinable within the new generation's psyche. ... One thing however should be pointed out: we are witnessing the reappearance, just as 50 years ago, of groups of young people who devote themselves body and soul to the revolutionary cause and who, in keeping with a tried-and-tested method, know how to wait for the right opportunities to trigger off or step up the unrest that they nonetheless continue to control, only to then go back into hiding, carry on undermining the foundations of society and plot other upheavals of a sporadic or extended nature as the case may be, with the aim of slowly disorganising the entire social structure' (Julien Freund, 'Guerres et paix' [Wars and Peace] (no. 4, 1968).

18. 'The admiring or later hostile exaggerations bandied about by all those who refer to us from the point of view of overzealous spectators should not be able to find legitimacy in a corresponding "situ-bravado" on our part that would promote the belief that the situationists are wondrous beings, every one of whose lives is actually blessed with everything they have articulated, or merely agreed with, in the way of revolutionary theory and agenda. ... The situationists have no monopoly to defend, nor any reward to expect. A task that suited us was undertaken, carried out through good and bad and, on the whole, properly, with the means available to us' (Guy Debord, note added to 'The Organisation

Question for the SI', *Internationale Situationniste*, no. 12, September 1969).

19. 'Theory becomes the ongoing knowledge of secret misery, of the secret of misery. It is therefore just as easily for itself the end of the spectacle effect. ... Living theory cannot therefore go wrong. It is a subject devoid of error. Nothing can mislead it. The totality is its one and only object. Theory knows misery to be a secretly public thing. It fully grasps the secret publicity of misery. It gives grounds for every hope. Class struggle exists' (Jean-Pierre Voyer, 'Reich, mode d'emploi' [(Wilhelm) Reich, directions for use], Éditions Champ Libre, Paris 1971, first translated as *The Use of Reich* (English translation by I. Ducasse Ltd, distributed by B.M. Piranha, London 1972). Thereafter as *Reich, How To Use* [July 1973] and included in *Public Secrets: Collected Skirmishes of Ken Knabb, 1970–1997*, Berkeley: Bureau of Public Secrets, 1997).

# Appendix 1
## Notes to serve towards the history of the SI from 1969 to 1971

As individuals express their life, so they are. What they are, therefore, coincides with their production, both with what they produce and with how they produce. (*The German Ideology*)

Getting on with members of one's own party is often more of a problem than acting against those forces hostile to it. (Cardinal de Retz, *Memoirs*)

The *Theses on the SI and its Time* reports what the SI has done since 1969 and all the reasons for what it has done. All we need do here is add a few succinct pieces of information on the main circumstances to be found over the same period; and on what became of a few individuals.

About a month before issue 12 of the French journal was published, Debord announced in a letter sent out on 28 July 1969 to all sections of the SI that this was the last issue for which he would be 'taking on the legal and editorial responsibility' of this journal's overall running. He called attention to 'the age-old revolutionary principle of the rotation of tasks', attaching 'all the more importance to it on this occasion, as many SI texts have been doing much to stress the coherence and the requisite abilities of all its members'. However, the kind of satisfaction on display here seemed to a large extent belied by the fact that as the membership of the French section increased, the newcomers had oddly enough taken to leaving the job of drawing up an ever greater share of the last few issues to Debord. Shortly afterwards, an editorial board was easily chosen to produce a subsequent issue on more collective lines; with everybody agreeing that such an issue should moreover bring about a renewal of the journal's form and content in keeping with the more complex and advanced conditions of practical activity that had by then developed. Thus the initial symptom of the crisis towards which the SI was fast heading went practically unnoticed in the mood of euphoria which was real enough on the part of many comrades, albeit a total sham where others were concerned.

The Venice Conference constituted a second, more visible and graver symptom. The eighth SI Conference was held in Venice from 25 September to 1 October 1969 with a very well-chosen building in the working-class district of la Giudecca home to its proceedings. These latter were constantly surrounded and monitored by a large number of informers of either the home-grown variety or else delegated by foreign police bodies. One part of this Conference was able to produce a sound analysis of revolutionary politics in Europe and America, and in particular predict the development of the Italian social crisis in the months to come, as well as the interventions that we would have to make in it. However, if such a debate was clear testimony to the most extremist and best informed political grouping then at work anywhere in the world, the best aspects of what the SI also represented in terms of critique, creation and basic theory in life as a whole, or simply in terms of the possibility of real dialogue between autonomous individuals – 'an association in which the free development of each is the condition for the free development of all' – proved to be entirely absent from the proceedings. In Venice, the 'pro-situ' mind-set was showcased in grandiose manner. Whereas a few comrades followed Vaneigem in maintaining a judicious silence throughout, half the participants spent three-quarters of the time restating in the strongest possible terms whatever the speaker before him had just come out with in the way of the same vague generalities, the entirety of conference proceedings meanwhile being translated into English, German, Italian and French. It became clear that the sole aim of each of these eloquent comrades was to point out that he was every bit as situationist as the next one; thus in a way justifying his presence at the Venice Conference, as though mere chance had led him to be there in the first place, yet equally well as though a subsequent, more historical justification were not foregone in the mere act of seeking this official recognition, which should by then have been considered a *fait accompli*. In short, for all that the 18 situationists there came up with, there might just as well have been four.

For more than a year after Venice, the French editorial committee consisting of Beaulieu, Riesel, Sébastiani and Viénet never succeeded in producing even 15 lines of usable copy. Not that what they penned was ever rejected by others, but quite simply because they themselves deemed what they wrote to be unsatisfactory. It should moreover be acknowledged that on this point they showed that they were lucid.

Mustapha Khayati who, in the latter years of the SI, had emerged as one of the most intelligent and able comrades, had submitted his resignation to the Venice Conference which, although accepting it, voiced deep disagreement over his future prospects. Two months earlier he had foolishly elected to play a part in the activities of the Popular Democratic Front for the Liberation of Palestine, within which he thought he could make out a revolutionary proletarian grouping; it is moreover common knowledge that under no circumstances can the SI brook a dual membership that would immediately border on manipulation. Khayati then went on to show in Jordan that he was less confident a revolutionary when he found himself isolated, in what was in actual fact a virtually hopeless situation, albeit one in which he had landed himself, than when he was well accompanied. Both the proletarian grouping within the PDFLP and even the slightest expression of its autonomous views had been purely and simply a figment of Khayati's well-intentioned imagination during his tenure on the mere executive of this miserable, underdeveloped leftist affair. All the Palestinian organisations were armed and enjoyed a position in Jordan of dual power, although the latter manifested itself strictly at the level of local conditions. Powerless, divided, yet increasingly enmeshed in bragging about their unity, the entire ludicrousness of the Arab States found its concentrated expression in the rudimentary, pseudo-machinery of State that shared the area of Jordanian territory which had gradually broken free from Hussein's rule. A dual power can never last, but be that as it may, none of the Palestinian organisations wished to overthrow Hussein, and so they all abandoned their one slim chance of success, unwilling even to see that the time had come to risk everything: the fact was that each one was afraid that the process might work to the advantage of some rival organisation and the Arab State protecting it. It was therefore perfectly obvious that Hussein would destroy the Palestinian organisations. You would have to be bound up in an ideological hysteria of the most undiluted sort not to see that few heads of state have managed time after time to show as much determination as King Hussein to stay in power at all costs, in the most difficult conditions, and not to see that he has the most dependable and loyal army of all the Arab countries at his disposal (which admittedly is not saying a lot, but was quite enough to weaken the ill-starred Palestinians whose obedience in military matters was to this kind of strategist). It was impossible for Khayati to be unaware of all this, but he was literally incapable of making the slightest comment about it. Nevertheless, the *boukha* having been drawn, it had to be drunk. Since the revolutionary Palestinian elements had merited Khayati's participation in their ranks, they also merited that before them he defend a minimum point of view, moreover that he serve warning to them. All he in actual fact did though was return to Europe a sorely disappointed man, prior to the inevitable crackdown. The subsequent period has of course seen him publish, on 1 August to be exact, and in conjunction with Lafif Lakhdar, 24 theses entitled *Waiting for the massacre* which notwithstanding did very little justice to the whole issue. It should be pointed out that this treatise, published in the Trotskyist news organ *An Nidhal*, was in fact written after the massacre which had begun before the summer and which by autumn had only required some finishing touches to be put to it. So then Khayati came to disappear once and for all from the SI; a departure scarcely designed, however, to bring him nearer to revolutionary praxis, and one that gave us no occasion to be upbeat about the mastery those comrades emerging from the tutelage of the SI are able to exercise within such praxis.

The SI's Italian section achieved far greater success in practical circumstances very nearly as dangerous; in particular by managing to elude the police who pretended to be looking for them in the wake of the bombings that were used by the Italian State security services in December 1969 to break or obstruct the movement of wildcat strikes, a movement that was then looking as though it would threaten in no time at all to undermine the foundations of society. They also managed there and then to publish and secretly distribute the pamphlet entitled *Il Reichstag brucia!* which lifted the lid on the key aspects of this ploy several months before the first tentative reservations concerning the affair began to be put forward by Italian leftists. The Venice Conference had foreseen the troubles of the months to come only too well, and had even stepped in to block the dispatch, designed to reinforce the Italian section, of a few 'French adventurers, an élite band of skirmishers one and all', to use the expression coined by the Loyal Servant at the time of other wars fought on Italian soil. On this occasion however it was the State that managed to step in and firmly seize the initiative (providing an instance of what could easily happen again elsewhere), leaving the Italian comrades to bear the obligation of temporary exile in France.

The whole turn of events discussed above then prompted us at the beginning of 1970 to embark on an orientation debate which was to determine the SI's future course of action, paying moreover particular attention to the methods it would employ, and to why some members were managing to do nothing. This debate, which lasted the best part of a year, clearly revealed the vacuous and abstract quality of the ideas to which many of the contemplative situationists cleaved, and even blew the lid off the naive tricks dear to particular individuals. Some confidently spoke of the need to do exactly what they themselves were incapable of doing, while others quietly went over and over various projects whose execution they had absolutely no intention whatsoever of undertaking. (The entire slew of mind-numbing documents and tiresome correspondence amassed by those who were incapable of doing anything else at that time may be consulted at the International Institute of Social History in Amsterdam.)

The coming to light of certain inadequacies and errors in the course of this debate or in matters of practical conduct saw, prior to the broader schism that we initiated in 1970, a number of SI members beaten into corners. Chevalier, Chasse and Elwell, Pavan, Rothe, Salvadori were excluded one after the other in relation to five separate matters which all bore on serious breaches of the SI's organisational procedures. Beaulieu and Cheval had to resign, albeit for very different reasons: Beaulieu because of the scorn his stupidity and lack of dignity were incurring, and Cheval because he had rounded off a drinking bout, from which he had emerged much the worse for wear than the others, by trying to defenestrate Sébastiani, whom he had not recognised and who was ultimately obliged to defend himself (it will be appreciated that an SI which brings an element of violence into play can at no time, for this very reason, allow violence to become established practice among its members). In conclusion, it should however be stressed that, despite the regrettable incidents that have obliged us to part company with them, Patrick Cheval, Eduardo Rothe and Paolo Salvadori are comrades we continue to hold in high esteem and who will doubtless be capable of making a significant contribution to the future stages of the revolutionary process unfolding at this present time. Not so the others.

These incidents, for the very reason that they had not removed solely, nor indeed all, the worst cases, in no way improved the quality of our thinkers or the vigour of our editors. Although everybody always rose as one in order to heap condemnation on those who had been excluded, many situationists continued to put up with one another, even though the very conditions they were experiencing made such tolerance look suspicious. Despite agreement on the fact that it was a matter of some urgency, the criticism of pro-situs was moving ahead no faster than that of the new period or the SI's real self-criticism. Those of us who did bring the most elements to bear on these tasks were approved in principle, without any of this actually being adopted and put to use. *Informations Correspondance Ouvrières*, a newspaper not usually noted for its enlightened opinions or truthfulness, even had the following eminently sensible remarks to offer the reader: 'The last two years have seen the entire corps of Vaneigemists very successfully curb the struggle for human adventure that the SI had been prosecuting for 15 years, within a given sphere, and by no means in isolation either. The struggle for daily life and on the basis of daily life, has been frozen into a *wretched, cosmetic makeover* of "certain" relationships, "certain" affinities, "certain" desires, combined in all three instances with the kind of apolitical attitude that can only make the Vaneigemists' "thirst for life" the subject of some doubt. As for their playful and creative capacities, anyone who has been privy to them will vouch for the fact that they in no way exceed those sported by the *bons vivants* we can all claim to be' (*ICO*, supplement to issues 97–98, undated).

Ever since the Venice Conference, and throughout this whole crisis, there had been agreement to the effect that the SI would be taking on no new members until it had clearly mastered the problems it was encountering in its own ranks. Doubtless matters might have reached a speedier conclusion if admission to the SI had been granted to a number of new comrades who would have immediately set about expelling the bunglers and *passé* individuals. This might however have presented the serious disadvantage of reinforcing the SI at a time when the most wide-ranging theoretical conclusions that could by then be roughed out with regard to this crisis and the new period convinced us rather that the best course of action lay in weakening the SI. It was moreover the case that, at least in the initial stages, such a procedure had by definition to involve a degree of subordination on the part of these new comrades to our views, for the purposes of a struggle that would see them triumph alongside situationists from several countries; added to which there is no longer any desire on our part to brook, even briefly, such subordination now that we have clearly seen what it is – and we saw it with such clarity precisely because the present time allows us to manage without it. These new members would therefore have constituted a step in the wrong direction, and the result itself an untimely one to which it would have led.

On the other hand, it was a good idea for the SI to say nothing for a while, especially in France. This served, first, to interrupt the conditioned reflex of a crowd of spectators – beyond a shadow of doubt a good half of our tens of thousands of readers – who simply longed to get their hands on the next issue of the journal they were now in the habit of consuming, so that they could update their 'knowledge' and their sham orthodoxy. But also because the SI had never written anything that ran secretly counter to what on the whole it was. At the time when the SI was *au fait* with a large part of its misery but had not yet overcome it, its silence avoided the unforgivable split between, on the one hand, writings that would seek to appear partly or wholly accurate and, on the other, the miserable state of affairs on the ground that would continue to go uncriticised: what some had sought to give sincere expression to in their writings in actual fact justifying the phoney existence of mute followers. A veiled split of this nature would not really suffer anything pertinent to be said about the Chinese bureaucracy or

American leftism; everything would be weighted by a factor of untruth. The SI thus preserved its integrity by saying nothing that might serve indirectly to cover up a lie or a grave uncertainty regarding itself. Doubtless many situationists, out of ruthless ambition or mere personal vanity, wished to carry on the glorious role of an SI that might have added a few choice pages to its style of yesteryear, after the odd partial criticism about the recent past or the latest expulsions; an SI moreover that might have evinced an improvement or a transcendence of which these situationists were not themselves the agents. However, the very people who might well have liked to keep up publications of this style were incapable of writing them. Those on the other hand who were equal to the task therefore let this inept crew get bogged down for some time, simply by taking the SI's organisational principles (each and every member's broad equivalence in terms of their abilities) at their word, the very principles it was now totally obvious could no longer in any way continue to be borne out with the likes of such people and in conditions such as these. This 'casting out the nines' demonstrated that what was wanting in the form was to an exact degree what was also wanting in the content. By gagging the SI in this way for what turned out to be rather a long time, we managed to reveal – first in a negative light – its crisis; and thus we began to help the thought and action of real autonomous forces to achieve freedom by dint of their own efforts. At a later stage, the end to the publication of a journal that was beginning to enjoy too conventional a success seems an even better idea to us. Other forms of situationist expression are more suitable for the new period. They will bring further disruption to bear on the routine of comfortably off spectators, who for their part will never know the answer to what they had most looked forward to finding out: which metallic colour had been chosen for the cover of issue 13? The journal that went by the name of *Internationale Situationniste* in France ran for 11 years (handled moreover by two printing firms in succession, the same period saw it bankrupt both of them). It dominated this period, and it achieved its aim. It played a key role in putting our ideas on to the contemporary agenda. The large number of pro-situ *aficionados* to whom the original purpose of this journal remains a complete and utter mystery – and who for their part seem, on the basis of all the talk about egalitarian autonomy that they put in in order to please us, to be quite incapable of coming up with anything on a par with it – no doubt fancied that they would continue to be supplied with their small dose of intellectual 'entertainment' – for the bargain sum of 3 francs to boot – right up to the end of the century. Well, that's what they thought! If they really want to read journals along those lines, they will have to start writing them themselves.

By the autumn of 1970, having been placed in the best experimental light, the historical impotence of the contemplative situationists had wholly rejoined its concept. They had to admit that revolutionary theory cannot be produced by ignoring the material foundations of existing social relations. This criticism of real, modern capitalism is what sets the SI apart not only from leftism as a whole, but also from the fabricated lyrical sighs of assorted Vaneigemists. We had to resume the critique of political economy by accurately understanding and combating 'the society of the spectacle'. And it certainly had to be kept up because since 1967 this society's downward spiral has continued apace. Those of the contemplatives who themselves knew that they were the sorriest cases – that is, the Beaulieus, Riesels and Vaneigems – and who consoled themselves by occasionally adopting, in the name of the SI, a condescending attitude towards a few individuals who, although outside our ranks, were often of far greater moment than they were, could neither reject the above task nor carry it out, and fell correspondingly victim to paralysis before the simplest activity. In the meantime, history continued – even for us! Added to which there was also no end of people to see, texts to read, letters to be written in ten different countries, translations to carry out, etc. The mere fact that we came into contact with those who could contribute nothing, or next to nothing to all these activities – or else produced little more than a botched effort – started to become a source of considerable irritation to us: their dogged and wearisome presence almost could have claimed to grab a share of the time of what they would term our amusements or profligacy (nor are the latter aspects of reality in any way at variance with the SI's outlook, although these things too remained qualitatively more or less beyond their reach). Besides, what left them particularly embittered was the fact that their status had been reduced to that of pure outsider in the context of everyday life, although this was where their moroseness became even more apparent than in the realm of political chatter. If 'boredom is counter-revolutionary', then the SI was very quickly succumbing to the same fate, without there ensuing as many protests as might have been expected.

On 11 November 1970 a new tendency was established within the SI which used the 'Declaration' promulgated on the same day to announce its intention of 'achieving a complete break with SI ideology', by means of 'a radical, that is, *ad hominem* critique', one refusing 'any reply which contradicts the actual existence of the person who frames it', and seeking culmination at the earliest possible opportunity in a 'split whose dividing lines will be determined by the forthcoming debate'. This new orientation declared itself moreover to be a first step and was in addition to carry on purges within its own ranks. Our 'Declaration' had an instant, practical success because it concluded with the announcement that we were going 'to make our positions known outside the SI'. The rout of the contemplatives began there and then.

Horelick and Verlaan, the last remnants of the American section, came out against a split. However for a split to be avoided, both sides need to have the same intention. Over and above the things that were demonstrably wrong with their practice and the claims they set forth in our organisational dealings with one another, we informed them that their involvement in our activities had at no point ever been important enough for us to be able to carry on taking equal responsibility for what they did. Even their secession elected not to appear as such for very long and, under the title *Create Situations*, they became an autonomous group in which Verlaan at least is mainly busying himself as American translator of past SI texts.

Vaneigem's bluff having been called, the content of his resignation letter (appended to the present volume) in which his clumsiness is as striking as his ignominy, was to reveal to the public what he had become. So the poor kid whose toy somebody has gone and broken exits in a bit of a huff: we get to hear that the SI had never been in the least bit interesting! So there! This twist nevertheless saw him recapture an originality that had long ago slipped from his grasp, albeit one standing completely on its head since he (for it just so happens that it is him ...) must be the only one in the world today who pretends that the disturbing historical and social question of the SI can be brushed aside with such cool and phoney contempt. It is easy to see why Vaneigem may now be wondering if the SI ever actually existed: 'The proof of the pudding is in the eating.' A certain period had seen Vaneigem write a revolutionary book, a book he could neither translate into practice nor amend in line with the subsequent advances of the revolutionary period. In such matters, a book's beauty can be judged only by that of its author's life. Moreover, whereas such a 'subjective' book – containing a wealth of rambling disclosures about himself and about what he needs, or would need, in the way of a more radical fix – could normally only represent the culmination of a life lived as much on the edge as to the full, all Vaneigem had done was write a preface to his non-existent life. Nowadays, in keeping with his one and only talent, as a man of letters, he writes prefaces to other people's works. In a communiqué entitled 'Concerning Vaneigem', drawn up by Debord and Viénet in the immediate aftermath of his resignation, the SI had publicly enjoined him to give details of at least one of the 'manoeuvring tactics' he claimed to have observed, tactics which he would obviously therefore have 'overlooked' the whole time he was with us. His silence was proof enough that the person concerned chose to admit his libel, rather than venture to defend it.

An altogether special mention however must be given to comrade Sébastiani. The two successive texts he sent to us at this time were characterised by an unquestionable honesty. In them he took himself to task over the fact that he had played nowhere near an active enough role, especially where writing was concerned. It would be remarkably petty of anybody though to censure Christian Sébastiani who, just prior to joining the SI, was the author of several of the SI's finest wall inscriptions – and who therefore articulated in a qualitatively distinguished way one of the most original aspects of this historical moment – for his laziness about putting pen to paper when the times were less volcanic. Our own criticism, which was to lead unfortunately to the end of our collaboration with him, bore on the fact that he had not really addressed the task incumbent upon him of steering a course for the SI himself; and that a theoretical grasp of the full extent of the afore-mentioned crisis, even when it was over, seemed always to escape him. We should also make it crystal clear that he cannot be identified with the conventional image of the pro-situ – or of the pro-situ member of the SI – in so far as this image has concealment, cowardice, pettiness in all aspects of behaviour, and more often than not ruthless ambition as its dominant features. Despite the fact that a nonchalance bordering at times on thoughtlessness can be laid at his door, with us Sébastiani has always been plain-dealing, brave and generous. His life has a dignity that commands respect, and his company much to recommend it.

Shortly after this split, René Viénet resigned in February 1971 for 'personal reasons'. Lastly, as if to lend the whole drama of civil strife and proscriptions within the SI something truly Shakespearian, the figure of the fool, to wit René Riesel, was in no way absent from the proceedings. For his part, Riesel had watched with glee as several rivals of his decided to call it a day, since he imagined that this would enable his own career to move forward. The new situation obliged him however to undertake various tasks for which nobody could have had less aptitude. A revolutionary at 17 – in 1968 – Riesel had the rare misfortune of growing old before his nineteenth birthday. Never had such a loser given himself over in so desperate a manner to such extremes of ruthless ambition, whose every means is denied him. He attempted to hide this ambitious streak, and the bitter envy that its continual frustration leads to, beneath that dodgy veneer of confidence proper to the weakling who, you know, lives in constant fear of a harsh word or a boot making contact with some part of his anatomy. At the time though, the only way he could make the cover-up of his sovereign inability to contribute anything to the SI's activities last a few weeks longer was by giving some people wretchedly misleading accounts of the way his non-existent endeavours were progressing or nearing completion. He had at the same time been quietly indulging in a few other bits of chicanery of the back shop and 'hand in the till' variety; and had even found himself having to go behind the backs of all but a select band of people he imagined were easy to fool, so as to endorse a few out-and-out lies that his ludicrous spouse was hawking around in an effort to enhance the image of her social standing, obviously spurred on by disgruntlement with the miserable reality of her domestic arrangements. Word very quickly got round about all this, as anybody but this second-rate crook could have seen was bound to be on the cards. Riesel had to come clean and was excluded in September 1971 as a consequence, in conditions that nobody, not even the Garnautin liars of 1967 had hitherto experienced.

Making a sudden reappearance therefore in the course of this purge of SI members was theoretical and practical activity which, along with its yield of pleasure, had been on the wane. The trivial and superficial aspects of this whole affair, and in particular the truly hilarious reality of many of those whose involvement cost them their tragic actor masks and subversive buskins, should not however skew our perception of the fact that what essentially obtained here, because the results bore on the SI and thus on a great many other people too, was a conflict over the most widespread conditions accompanying present-day revolutionary struggles, as well as over history itself.[*]

[*] This text and the following one are by Guy Debord. (Publisher's note, Éditons Fayard)

**THE REAL SPLIT IN THE INTERNATIONAL**

# Appendix 2
## On our enemies' decay

A secret power having refused us the Cleveland Hall rooms, the meeting took place at the Bell Tavern, Old Bailey, under citizen Besson's chairmanship. The meeting was a well-attended and spirited affair. In one speech after another, citizens Besson, Weber, Paintot, Prévost, Kaufman, Denempont, Lelubez, Holtporp and Debord vigorously proclaimed the rights of the people, to the applause of those assembled. (Communiqué issued by the London French Branch of the International Workingmen's Association; collected in 'International Workingmen's Association', document published by the imperial police, Paris, 1870)

In the 'Theses' that go to make up the present volume, we have endeavoured to lay bare not only *the deep historical foundations* of the activity pursued by a movement like the SI, but also the links that must in point of fact have existed between these foundations, our theory, our strategy and even the particular charm that the most effective part of our language, and of our actual lives, brought quite naturally into play. Only at this level of understanding is it possible to discover the secret of the historical *success* underpinning such movements, which by way of its proof to the contrary, sheds an all-pervasive light on the conditions in which thousands of other attempts have met with failure. Our enemies however – bourgeois historians, police officers, high-ranking bureaucrats, moderate pro-situs of the contemplative school, leftists in possession of various minor hierarchical organisations – totally misunderstood the whole issue. First and foremost they see *the term* 'situationist' as empirically corresponding to the actions and viewpoints of the most radical of today's revolutionary proletarians, both in factory and in school – that is, of the most clear-cut and formidable enemies they have. Instead of trying to come up, on the basis of this scientifically indisputable observation, with a straightforward explanation of the phenomenon, they prefer in actual fact to cast any such explanation aside by attaching a ludicrously overblown importance to the mere *label*. Their immediate concern is to tack on a distinct form of pernicious ideology, fully the rival of their own efforts, to this situationist label and which, even *qua* ideology, is a particularly lame and muddled affair *since it is the purely fanciful creation of those who are locked in combat with it* (it is moreover safe to say that the latter no longer even have anything remotely approaching the intellectual resources with which their nineteenth-century predecessors were blessed when it comes to even the dishonest refutation of opposing views). The path they follow at this point runs into an insuperable difficulty: how is it possible for so narrow-minded and so stupid an ideology to arouse so much enthusiasm and proceed in irritating fashion to rise up before them as a practical force? They hold that this is purely and simply down to the warped minds and shocking exploits of the SI's 'leaders' – who would for their part have taken malicious pleasure or found some dubious advantage not only in casting a slur on the perfection attained by the society that the former represent, but also in driving those who admire it to despair, whether this society be the fine commodity abundance of the West or the tough bureaucratic discipline of the East, or simply the moth-eaten images of those stillborn revolutions that aspire to replace the teams responsible for managing the whole thing. The fact that this explanation, whose every term is *fuelled by indignation*, immediately ends up conferring a literally titanic, historically transcendent power on a few situationist ringleaders, does nothing to deter our enemies. They would much rather acknowledge that they are being held up to ridicule as a result of the worldwide plot of a handful of individuals than admit that they are quite simply being held up to ridicule *by the times in which they live*. They must be wondering then *who* exactly is aiding and abetting the said plot. Neither able nor indeed willing to grasp that present-day historical conditions and the proletariat are the sole villains of the piece, some will identify the culprit as East Berlin or Havana, while at the same time others will say that those who have chosen so unwisely to give their wholehearted backing to the Situationist International are big capital and neo-fascism. Whether bourgeois, bureaucrats or spectators, our enemies can conceive of history only in the form of spectacular, organisational or police manipulations (to name but a few types) which are those of the anti-historical period we have just left behind, and which they themselves, including the most left-leaning or supposedly 'anarchist' elements among them, have never once stopped using as far as their circumstances allowed. By grounding their thinking in this kind of speculative approach, one that moreover affords them a greater or lesser degree of reassurance, and by contending that the situationist elements who come to the fore in some wildcat strike or other, in some illustration or other of the way rebel youth behaves, in some riot that escapes the control of those who nursed every hope of containing it, or in some act of sabotage directed against the 'best' hierarchical organisation advocating leftist revolutionary principles, are perforce always activists controlled by the SI or infiltrated on our orders, our enemies demonstrate they have zero understanding of the SI and of the times in which they themselves live. They cannot even grasp that it is more often than not *through their own clumsy mediation* that these revolutionary elements, whom they denounce and hunt down, have themselves managed to catch on to the fact that they 'were' situationist; and that this, in a word, is how the present age has come to term *what they are.*

'This was the first time that the disturbing figures of the Situationist International appeared. How many of them are there? Where do they all come from? Nobody seems to know.' Ever since its appearance in the *Républicain Lorrain* of 28 June 1967, this angst-ridden discovery has set the tone for *the reactionary view* of an entire period of struggles.

If the police are legitimately rankled by their own failure to infiltrate, as they do elsewhere, observers into the SI, left-wing organisations fret quite mistakenly over an imaginary infiltration of situationists wielding the most corrupt influence within these leftist ranks. The fact is that both the SI and the present age carry on their corrupting influence in another way entirely, although it is not hard to see why leftists turn out to be the ones most incensed at this phenomenon: for down among 'their public', that is, among the pick of the individuals and groups that they seek to ensnare, is the very place they come across their old enemy: proletarian autonomy in the early stage of asserting itself. They unwittingly pay us, moreover, the special tribute of denouncing this autonomy as being *under our influence*. The genuine propensity to experience our influence to some degree would of course be in perfect keeping with its very essence: it rejects all other influence and is unlikely ever to experience ours as some command or other. Proletarian autonomy can only be influenced by its time, its own theory and its own action.

The most extreme and quite the most fanciful example of this obsession with the struggle against the SI, acknowledged as the main task facing the most 'extremist' organisations, was no doubt furnished by the Carrara Congress of the Italian Anarchist Federation held in April 1971. This Anarchist Federation can hardly be said to loom large in Italian working-class circles, but on the other hand Italy currently finds itself in a pre-revolutionary situation. What then does this Federation see as the most urgent theoretical and practical task before it? Put briefly: to combat the SI and eradicate SI members from its ranks, in which none of them have ever served or even, of course, have ever had the slightest involvement. *Nevertheless it was* *upon the above task that all the proceedings of the Tenth FAI\* Congress quite openly came to focus;* this, together with the fact that all the preparations for the said Congress, that is, not only the public controversies but also the infighting between the leadership and loyal or insurgent activists, were dominated by this signal item of business. The only 'theoretical' and political document to come out of this Congress, an editorial entitled 'Situationists and Anarchists' published by the FAI Correspondence Commission in the 15 May 1971 issue of its journal *Umanità Nova*, is in fact concerned with this and nothing else.

'The press was in due course informed', this communiqué nobly begins, 'of the decision taken by the anarchists to exclude "situationists" – sometimes wrongly referred to as "anarcho-situationists", "Bordighist-situationists", "council communists", "wildcats", etc. from the Tenth Congress of the Italian Anarchist Federation (held in Carrara, 10–12 April). The motion carried unanimously by the anarchists assembled at the Congress warrants further explanation.' Without knowing who all the above people are, it will not by now have gone unnoticed that, as far as actual situationists are concerned, the FAI might just as well have excluded anyone belonging to the Sioux, former officers with the Imperial Indian Army, Black Panthers and the Anthropophagi: it would not have registered a single departure among its members after that.

---

\* FAI: Federazione Anarchica Italiana, not to be confused with the famous Federación Anarquista Ibérica. (Publisher's note)

Let us now take a look at the explanations: 'Ever since the years 1967–68 the influence of the Situationist International, deployed to particularly negative effect on many Scandinavian, North American and Japanese extra-parliamentary groupings, has been used in France and Italy to destroy both these latter countries' federated anarchist movements, in the name of a theoretical exposé that the situationists routinely swamp in a tide of insolence and vague, convoluted sentences.' These anarchists are nevertheless good enough not to lay the further charge of cooking up a few other schemes actually within parliament at our door. What will be wondered at, though, are the finely honed and far from convoluted sentences with which these poor souls put themselves at the centre of the world, and quite confidently credit us with the ludicrous aim of taking an interest in people like them.

After the above stab at revealing our essence, here they are showing the latter's realisation in an historical form: 'Situationism issued from the fertile imagination of a group of intellectuals who, in 1957, convened round a table for a debate on art and urbanism, decided to use their cultural contacts to found a political, pseudo-revolutionary movement, a kind of "revolutionary" movement steeped in *Qualunquismo*.' A glimpse here, then, of where debate about art and urbanism, and perhaps debate in general, could lead were the FAI not around to spare people all these intellectual liberties. These parish priests go even further than the Stalinists who, as long as leftists are not in their prisons, by and large simply maintain either that the latter play 'objectively' into capitalism's hands, or that they are being manipulated despite their naive good will. The *perverse intent* guiding the SI's founders is perceived here as given from the outset. In post-war Italy, '*Qualunquismo*', or 'party of the man-in-the-street' was in fact the name behind which former fascists and neo-fascists hid. What dangerous artists though! Never has the 'imagination' that drives men to repudiate dogmas and to transform the world had more appalling consequences, in so far at any rate as its actual centre, in the shape of the FAI, is concerned. And to crown it all, the whole business was decided 'round a table' – thus is the full extent of the crime revealed! *It would appear then that we had a table* – but nothing whatsoever to do with one another or any sort of 'cultural contacts'. The table seems, in addition, to be more than enough to prove our evil nature and to warrant our being identified, a bit further on, with 'the young jet-set'. This anarchist conclave, which seems to display a clear-cut preference for the rostrum, or the pulpit as the case may be, is unaware of the fact that probably the most important share of human activity, if we accept that the bed deserves to be put in a category of its own, has always taken place around tables ever since the first one was invented. These malicious idiots are nothing if not dogged though: 'Well aware however that the coexistence of a Situationist International with other revolutionary political movements, and especially with the anarchist movement is impossible, they decided ...' It is worth noting at this point that we have never envisaged the existence of the 'anarchist movement', only that of present-day realities. It is nevertheless true that we hold the SI's views to be incompatible in the long term with the existence and claims of 'other revolutionary political movements', for the simple reason, moreover, that if the wretched anarchist bureaucracy does go trailing after these unspecified 'other political movements' nowadays, the quality of 'revolutionary' movement is not something we for our part recognised in them; and everything that has happened since merely confirms us in our opinion. But what, according to the 1971 class of the FAI, did the situationists decide in 1957? 'They decided that first and foremost their task would be to infiltrate the other revolutionary political movements [NB yet another reference to this majestic multitude who act as our foil] in order to destroy them with accusations of support for ideological and organisationally tinged bureaucratic doctrines, not to mention their indiscriminate use of slander and provocation to this end.' There can be little doubt about what rankles them: the SI has become the bad conscience of ideologues and bureaucrats, each and every one of whom is encountering opposition within *their own sphere of influence*. As for slander and provocation, anybody would think they were reading *The Protocols of the Elders of Zion*, since nobody anywhere has ever been able to cite a single example of an SI member infiltrating any kind of organisation. FAI police and judges would no doubt respond to this with a gasp of incredulity, as would the thousands of our agents they have been busy unmasking everywhere, and 'especially' within their own organisation! These paranoiacs merely do a more stupid job of articulating the torment that so many other bureaucratic organisations try more discreetly to exorcise.

Yet on they go, settling the muddled issue of the SI's actual organisation along the way. Whereas so many others criticise us, wrongly moreover, for tending to act on pure impulse whatever the circumstance, and for being hostile to any organisational agreement reached by proletarians, the Italian Anarchist Congress can reveal that: 'Their critique of ideologies and organisations does not, however, apply to their own ideology or to their own hierarchical organisation. The latter is based on national sections and (apparently autonomous, randomly labelled) local groups, which are in actual fact the cover for a political nerve-centre comprising a small number of intellectuals who have financial means of unknown provenance at their disposal as and when they need it.' What artists! It must be admitted that FAI bosses have more than enough reason to be terrified, finding themselves exposed to the hostility of such unscrupulous and well-resourced *condottieri*. It may already be gathered from their righteous indignation that they themselves will never sink to the fanatical depths of a Nechaev and that, if they run their FAI along bureau-cratic lines, it will be something akin to the PSU* and not modelled on Bakunin's 'International Brotherhood' or on Durruti's group in the Spanish CNT.** However, if this point is an absorbing one for those people with an interest in the prevailing *doctrinal* conceptions of the latest stage of Italian anarchism, in no way does it apply to the SI, and nothing therefore that might serve either to censure us or endorse us can be got from the pipe dreams entertained by these individuals on this score. What could hardly go unnoticed either, in the course of their pronouncements,

---

* PSU: Parti Socialiste Unifié. (Translator's note)
** CNT: Confederación Nacional de Trabajo. (Translator's note)

is the age-old Stalinist, and even more time-honoured counter-revolutionary argument of 'financial means of unknown provenance'. Of course, if we had needed particularly large sums of money and if we had in fact managed to get our hands on them, their provenance would doubtless remain unknown to the FAI's policemen. But where has evidence that we had any 'financial means' ever been unearthed? Nowhere else, it would appear, than by counting the thousands of agents we were hiring throughout the world to disturb not only Brezhnev's, but also the FAI's, Nixon's and the principality of Monaco's rest in a wholly impartial way! By crediting us with the authorship of 'varied and costly publications of an international and local character' whose financial origin seems to them to be 'incredibly suspect', they pretend to entertain the belief that we have to foot the bill for 50 per cent of the myriad anti-establishment publications that have been continually rolling off the presses in the smallest European and American towns over the last two or three years. By way of putting the record straight here, we now have a dozen publishers, with some of them even going so far as to pay us royalties. As for the journals we have been publishing entirely at our own expense, albeit in nowhere near the numbers hinted at above, they quickly managed to attract such a large readership that they were starting to be commercially viable, despite their low cover price. It was at this point, however, that we decided not to rest on laurels like these, and halted the most famous publication. In a word, history, and not some cabal, is now undermining the old world of leftism.

'Situationism is a very far cry from the world of work, according to these people that the world of work sends packing, in the same way that the anarchists are a far cry from the young situationist jet set who – either knowingly or unwittingly, honestly or dishonestly – wish to play the part of counter-revolutionary *agents provocateurs* ...' And just for good measure, they maintain that 'five ashen-faced representatives of the Situationist International in Italy' were behind an attack on an FAI bureaucrat which took place 'on the evening of 14 April' in Florence; they furthermore insinuate that around this time we were also involved in the activities of a gang that burned down the offices of an Italian fascist newspaper, our sole aim being of course to do our bit in a crackdown on anarchists. Finally, and still in the name of the 'world of work', they condemn the Reggio di Calabria rebels: deeds of this kind 'are not, as the situationists contend, the revolutionary indication of a proletariat accomplishing the self-management of its daily life. Rather they are *Sanfedist* indications ...' Sanfedism was a mass movement, steered by the clergy, against the French troops of the First Republic occupying the kingdom of Naples. It would thus be about as serious as suggesting that this whole, sorry FAI Congress is the expression of a Girondist federalism bribed by Pitt's gold. In the pamphlet entitled *Gli operai d'Italia e la rivolta di Reggio Calabria* [The workers of Italy and the revolt of Reggio di Calabria] (Milan, October 1970), which met with enormous success everywhere and, thanks to other rebels, went through several reprints abroad, the SI had alone rallied to the defence of Reggio's proletarians whose name was being blackened by the government, the

Stalinists and all shades of leftism. After a while, many leftists had a change of heart, if not an outright change of political allegiance, and even Italian Stalinists ended up to a very large degree having to tone down their initial condemnations. This whole issue sees the FAI alone remain unswervingly loyal to the Christian Democrat government, an FAI who moreover elect to insult us by slandering Calabrian workers with all the gusto that it employed in describing the SI.

The anarchists of the FAI are not merely loathsome and ludicrous in their own right; they like to think they are *exemplary*. At the same time that they publicly give us away to the police – hardly an earth-shattering development since the latter already know from experience that evidence supplied by its paid informers within these anarchist circles does not stand up in court – they set about teaching their leftist colleagues the right way to ward off evil: 'The decision adopted by the FAI Congress effectively pulls the plug on the situationists' [NB which was like pulling a thirty-third tooth out of us, or removing our right to sit in the Hungarian Parliament] chances of ever refining their attempts at incitement to rebel, in the first instance within the ranks of the FAI itself, and in so far as these attempts at incitement could well serve as an example to local groups and federations with or without FAI affiliation, whose ranks the situationists try to infiltrate in order to lead them down the road to ruin with the aid of a combination of ideological confusion and the exercise of systematic contradiction very strongly reminiscent of Sorelian chauvinism, hidden beneath the principles of violence for violence's sake.' One can just imagine, as if omnipresence were our forte, these situationists who simply infiltrate everywhere, 'looking for whoever they can swallow up' and whoever can be led down the road to ruin, thanks to their *anti-ideological* dialectic and their exercise of systematic contradiction which by and large affords them a quite uncanny resemblance *to history itself*. For each and every one of society's owners, even badly off ones with nothing but the FAI to their name, these situationists represent *historical evil*. It should furthermore be pointed out that if in France Georges Sorel is known rather more as a theorist of revolutionary syndicalism, he has a very different reputation in Italy owing to the fact that the early supporters of Mussolini claimed to draw their inspiration from him.

As in so many other cases, if the ludicrous FAI had no situationist in its ranks, it was bound to produce some with its stupid crackdown. As always, it is moreover *in the wake of* confrontations of this kind within sects we know absolutely nothing about that certain elements see fit to get into contact with us, and privately furnish us with loathsome 'confidential' documents of an internal nature that were used by the FAI leadership as a basis for their Congress proceedings, and in fact yielded nothing but the rift with those who felt they could no longer back the FAI's stupid and slanderous remarks. Perusal of these documents turns up the following confession with its curious pessimism: 'Driving out situationists from our groups will guarantee that these very groups survive.' One of these documents refers personally to 'Sanguinetti, SI representative for Italy', as the secret agent who took a direct hand in organising the opposition to and the break-up of the aforementioned Carrara Congress.

As for the unqualified and blanket hatred that 'every representative of the old world and every political party' have developed for him, comrade Sanguinetti has managed in the course of 1971 alone to clinch a kind of record that every revolutionary may wish they held. He was very nearly killed in Milan when Stalinist heavies tried to run him over in their cars, a murder that was only just prevented by the quick action of workers in the vicinity. For its part, the FAI has marked him out, albeit this time in a far more academic way, as the enemy of anarchy and somebody to get rid of. Finally, on 21 July, the Minister of the Interior had him promptly expelled from France, despite the fact that he has never been domiciled there, on the sole grounds that his continued presence in Paris would be highly prejudicial to State security.

It is true that all the FAI's *show* did was to epitomise a set of counter-situationist myths which are everywhere the product of the same self-interested confusionism and the same helplessness. Anyone reading the December 1970 issue of a modernist rag entitled *Actuel*, intellectual pollution's very own house-magazine of sorts, could, among a dozen other fanciful concoctions, have come across the same old imagery conjuring up the SI's *invisible empire*, if not the Revolution's very own Ku Klux Klan: 'Police forces throughout Europe hold files on them and hunt them down. In their capacity as elusive and covert plotters of the time-honoured variety, they reject all legal restraints and conformist principles, even socialist ones. The practice of fellowship towards other leftist groups is not one these outlaw aristocrats of the revolution go in for.' Although it is unclear whether his was an hereditary elevation or one that came via the ballot-box, these aristocrats could not fail to come up with their king in the person of Guy Debord: 'He is a little man with a face like a schoolteacher's and a line in badly-cut jackets. ... He is becoming more and more obsessed with his enemies as he gets older, uncovering treachery and scandal everywhere; combating enemies is not exactly his style though, since he would much rather wipe them off the face of the earth. *The Society of the Spectacle*, a one-off, jerky disquisition, is his only known book.' Doubtless the physical description given here will scarcely provide those who 'are hunting us down' with much to go on, since it is quite obvious that this journalist has never set eyes on Debord, added to which there seems to be some uncertainty as to whether he has any idea what schoolteachers look like nowadays. Permeating these lines to the highest degree possible, however, are the age-old, secular myths of revolutions and their leaders, recounted in true bourgeois style with its 'where there's muck, there's brass' leitmotif. The nonsense of the dead weighs heavily upon the brains of living idiots. The little, nondescript man, to whom nobody would give so much as a second look, is Blanqui – the 'Old Man' who owes all his implacability and fearsomeness to the fact that he is surrounded by loyal fanatics ready for just about anything. The image also has a good dash of Trotsky through it and, were drugs and political assassination to put in an appearance, maybe the 'Old Man of the Mountain' too. Elsewhere, mark if you will the terms 'one-off, jerky disquisition' used to denote a book of theory that the hack would on no account have been capable of reading: but that's Marat! Busy uncovering treachery everywhere and committed to wiping his enemies off the face of the earth, it must surely be out of a concern to spare people rivers of blood that Debord is urging you to sacrifice a few drops, 100,000 severed heads, or why not, in these inflationary times, five times that number. It is no bad thing if revolutionaries show less and less leniency: so many others end up toeing the line more and more as they get older, and some of them have in fact only ever pretended to reject anything at all. In the case of Debord though, his dreadful reputation for severing ties with, and expelling, people was already well established 20 years ago when he was 20 (and is a point made by all those who have written about him; cf. Asger Jorn and even Jean-Louis Brau). It must be admitted therefore that 'as he gets older' – doubtless prematurely worn-out by continual orgies – the chances of him dealing treacherously with anybody will have been reduced to nil!

Books are appearing in Germany, America, Holland and Scandinavia that all look with admiration on the SI's activities in the years prior to May 1968, stopping only to deplore the fact that all this fine potential – grasped chiefly in terms of the role that such-and-such a long-excluded situationist in a particular locality subsequently managed to play to poorer effect in the early stages of German or Dutch protest movements – has been continually and ruthlessly cut short by what a recent Swedish book of *Nashist* history (two words that to all intents and purposes cancel each other out) calls 'General Debord's' dictatorship, which has relentlessly overseen the continual exclusion of all and sundry. What is still required, however, is an understanding of how and why it has been possible to accomplish so much using these methods; and why it was Debord, and not Jørgen Nash, the Garnautins or the Vaneigemists who had a stream of candidates for exclusion constantly to hand, with never any let-up in membership turnover or in members' willingness to take their exit. Is there not some *concretely historical* reason for this? What, moreover, is the point of talking about authoritarian prestige when it is common knowledge that Debord has always been besieged by a great many people wishing to be of some kind of service, and that on each occasion he has acted swiftly to turn nearly every single one of them away? Thus for their part, those who look to a few narrow observations drawn from so-called 'psychological reflection' to explain everything will forever find themselves stumped by the following mystery: why has success in diabolically netting all these people fallen to him then? And why, given his success, have they been ready to follow him wherever he chose to take them?

This whole area is a breeding ground for other, lesser concoctions that serve above all to pad out all manner of hackwork. Some books have Debord's birthplace as Cannes, which is probably, after Paris, the start of a list of seven cities in France that will be boasting this highly debatable honour. A story that continues to be touted in publications as far afield as America, presents Debord as the heir of an extremely wealthy industrialist – whereas it is plain to see that he has led a life teeming with adventure, and that he had to formulate his critique of political economy even before running into his Engels. With the same idea of reducing the worrisome unknown to a reassuring known, it is alleged just about everywhere that Debord could only be an *agrégé* in philosophy, whereas he is nothing of the kind, and not even attached to the CNRS.* Neither is he, despite all the rumours, series editor with Éditions Champ Libre.

It is simply not possible for every pro-situ, labouring under the hail of insults described above, to remain in ever-lasting awe of the SI; and when they find themselves forced to join the ranks of our detractors, they occasionally outdo the FAI in ludicrousness. What have we not been upbraided for? Some of them claim we manipulated not only the crowds on the May 1968 barricades but also the Sorbonne assemblies. They further allege that we successfully led progressive Glaswegian workers astray, and corrupted Parisian hoodlums. There are claims too that we have exercised a pernicious influence over wildcat strikers at the Fiat plant in Turin, as well as over the most radical of the armed Palestinian units (*supra* for details of the skilled go-between concerned). If the latter waited blindly to be slaughtered, then it was because of us; and without us, the Kiruna miners would perhaps have liberated the very first territory for the Councils inside the Arctic circle. Without us, the workers of Reggio would not have taken up arms; or else they would have brought down the Italian State within 48 hours. On the one hand, we are reported to have well-nigh fomented all the unrest that has become such a feature of modern society; while on the other, our hidebound and

---

* CNRS: Centre National de la Recherche Scientifique. (Translator's note)

ever clumsy directives are supposed to have automatically led to its every single failure. Let's just leave it there.

Owing to the fact that it occupies a position of rather more practical consequence, asinine impudence is taken to even greater heights by those publishers who are to be found wavering and torn between, on the one hand, the hatred we quite rightly fill them with, and on the other their wish to make a bit of extra money, or even to mount a desperate rescue attempt on their sorry reputations by publishing us now. Towards the end of 1971, Feltrinelli Editore wrote to us to request foreign language rights to the SI journal. The somewhat cool terms of our reply made it clear that we had no wish to be published by the Stalinist Feltrinelli, whereupon a man called Brega, the director of the publishing house in question, wrote back to recommend we see a psychiatrist for turning down such an offer, to inform us that the very terms of our refusal smacked of 'stupid arrogance' and to tell us that Feltrinelli has never been a Stalinist. So many falsehoods! This Brega pretends to be surprised that, after regularly indicating in our journal that all the material therein is copyright-free, we were slipping back into what he himself is not afraid to call 'the beaten track trodden by overground publishing and bourgeois authors'. Thus it was that the SI's reply to this saw it adopt a somewhat tougher line: 'A turd like you would like to be in the very position once occupied by Stalin so that you too can lay down the accepted definition of words *all by yourself*. Feltrinelli, you say, is no Stalinist; in that case neither is Dubček, nor Kádár, nor Arthur London, nor Castro, nor Mao Zedong. Nor, for that matter, could you yourself Brega be dismissed as a bastard and a fool. We well understand your stake in all this but get real! … If anybody is in the habit of playing bourgeois legal games, your publishing house is – witness your request for foreign language rights from us, not to mention the fact that it is precisely because of everything you represent that *we have chosen to withhold them from you*. If our contempt is a matter of indifference to you, *bella fica, you should never have approached us with any request in the first place*. For their part, revolutionaries have always managed to reprint anything they like in the way of writings by the SI; and we have never raised the slightest objection to the numerous pirate editions of our texts and books in a good many countries. But Feltrinelli & Co. are not even worthy of pirate editions. Moreover, should your firm choose in point of fact to disregard our refusal, you can rest assured we will not be countering such a move through any proper or bourgeois channels. Since you had the gall to push yourself forward with this letter, we would regard you, Gian Piero Brega, as not only *personally* to blame for the publication of our texts in any way, shape or form by Feltrinelli, but also as the person we would take it out on.' (This exchange of letters was immediately printed and posted up in Italy under the title 'Corrispondenza con un editore'.) There are bound therefore to be suggestions from some quarters that the SI blew up Feltrinelli a few days later with dynamite. There were even claims in the *Corriere d'Informazione* of the 18–19 March that the SI had been demanding an initial payment of no less than *1 billion lira* in protection money from Feltrinelli, a state of affairs best summed up thus: 'From that to murder, there is only one step.' In the spring of 1971, the third print run of *The Society of the Spectacle* saw Éditions Buchet-Chastel unilaterally and unexpectedly take the liberty of adding a *subtitle*: 'Situationist theory'. This addition, whose inclusion is an infringement of standard editorial practice – and even directly contravenes established bourgeois law – was, as it turns out, all the more monstrous in view of the fact that the word 'situationist' is used *only once* in the course of this book (in thesis 191), with the very deliberate intention of making a distinction between us and the host of would-be revolutionaries who imagined they were guaranteeing the radicality of their prose by larding it with quotes from, and good words for, the SI. As may be gathered from the above remarks, it is not our style to become in any way a party to the whole sphere of bourgeois law by instituting proceedings against Buchet-Chastel that would have led unquestionably to a judgement in our favour. A more dignified solution was to have *La Société du spectacle* reissued by another Paris-based publisher; which is what Éditions Champ Libre offered to see to there and then. One result of this we have since been able to witness is a quaint little caper that involved the publisher-forger putting his case before the courts, and obtaining an injunction ordering the seizure of the entire stock of the genuine article as published by Éditions Champ Libre. However, this will not of course be enough to bring either this book or its author back to its first publisher. The French edition, since reprinted in Holland, along with the translations published in the USA, Denmark and Portugal, have all refused to recognise the claims currently being pursued in relation to royalties and fair trading by Buchet-Chastel (hence the only thing that the latter will have managed to come up with is the Italian edition published by Di Donato, comprising a translation so riddled with errors that it is bound to be rivalled before long by a pirate edition of greater accuracy).

With the benefit of a few years' hindsight, the 1968 occupations movement has, in the eyes of everybody – and even its enemies who are the slowest to admit it but not to feel the effects of it – taken its place in the long line of French revolutions: thanks to the basic outline it provided, the main features of modern revolution, its true content, have been well and truly brought out into the public arena. Moreover, as time goes by, it will be necessary for future books on May 1968 to devote more and more room in their discussions to the SI. For the moment however, this is a field where mythical invention still holds sway. In spite of the fact that the book by Raspaud and Voyer, *L'Internationale situationniste*,[*] can be singled out as the one study deserving of unqualified praise because of the seriousness of its approach, the latter remains purely a chronological and biographical one, without ever venturing into the specifically historical aspect. Many of these books, like the idiotic *Image-action de la société* (Éditions du Seuil, 1970),[**] hawked up by Alfred Willemer and his team

[*] Jean-Jacques Raspaud and Jean-Pierre Voyer, *L'Internationale situationniste: chronologie/bibliographie/protagonistes (avec un index des noms insultés)* (Paris: Éditions Champ Libre, 1972). (Translator's note)
[**] Alfred Willemer, *The Action-Image of Society: On Cultural Politicization*, trans. A.M. Sheridan Smith (New York: Pantheon Books, 1970). (Translator's note)

of two-bit sociologists, try and draw a distinction between the situationists, as brilliant precursors and theoreticians, and those in 1968 who were actually in the practical movement. Thus the old scholastic distinction between those who 'give expression' to an historical movement and those who put it into action is wheeled out anew. However the principal scandal that these researchers would like to cover up is the fact that the very same situationists were actually present on the barricades, at the Sorbonne, in the factories – locations in which we developed *the theory of the moment itself*. Even within those groves of Academe devoted to it, and even, for that matter, in the hands of better researchers than Adrien Dansette and Alfred Willemer, history will find nothing better in the way of texts revealing such a sound grasp of the event and a clearer anticipation of the consequences *from day to day and for an entire historical period* than the main writings circulated in large numbers at that time by the SI and the 'Council for maintaining the occupations' – in particular the 'Address to All Workers', thousands of copies of which we sent abroad immediately after its publication on 30 May 1968, it being a document we had then looked upon, regardless of the possible outcome of events, as the *testament* of the entire occupations movement. The age-old academic dispute to ascertain the extent to which history can ever be *foreseen* by those who live through it has been settled *once again* here by revolutionary experience. The revolutionary moment *concentrates* the entire historical potential of society as a whole into a mere three or four propositions whose gradual evolution in terms of power struggles, growth or overthrow can clearly be witnessed; whereas in the general run of things, society's *routine* is unpredictable – except in its general truth where it can be recognised as specific *predetermined* routine, and where it is consequently possible to foresee the main outline of its future direction – because this very routine is the product of an infinite number of *scattered* processes whose individual growth and interaction are impossible to calculate in advance. It is at such moments that those who regularly spend every waking hour of the day not thinking, start to think in accordance with an everyday logic. Leftists saw only the Smolny Institute all over again, or the Long March, and thus ended up even more clumsy-looking in the Paris of 1968 than they might have been, without Lenin, at Smolny. The masses felt that what was already to hand was the possible transformation of their lives. However, of all the leftists who were volunteering their opinions in the movement's assemblies, there was not one single one who had the slightest idea, not only of what would come next, but also of what *could* come next (many never even gave so much as a thought to *how close* we then came to a full-scale crackdown when the movement subsided). Thus the ludicrous dialectic of the leftist and the spectacle is something we have been treated to in France ever since. Each time that the spectacle must once again begin to admit that workers are continually becoming more subversive, it pretends to rediscover the crucial role played by leftists in bringing about this unfortunate result; indeed, its experience in throwing the blame on to leftists tends, if anything, to buoy up the spectacle. It is in fact common knowledge that all the left-wing parties put together do not control even a tenth of the

150,000 people who took to the streets for the funeral of Pierre Overney.[*] Leftism has, over the course of the last four years, shown the full extent of its otherworldly lack of realism. It is an ongoing, scandalous fact, moreover, that all the left-wing parties, with the exception of the Maoists but including the French anarchist 'organisations' who toe the same line as their Italian counterparts, are *very careful not to do anything* that might offend the official Stalinist party. The Maoists – it need hardly be pointed out that the bits of 'Situationism' that they frequently mix into their revolutionary gruel can neither be understood nor used by them, indeed *any more than Marxism can* – quite openly vilify this party, albeit in the name of *another Stalinism* – one moreover of a particularly pseudo-Chinese cast – which is far more bellicose, yet even more decayed than the bureaucratic conservatism of a Georges Marchais[**] is; and which invariably makes itself look ridiculous as it seesaws from 'people's courts' to 'people's prisons', without for a moment ever managing to grasp what is actually happening in France or worldwide. Political pundits as well as the so-called Communist Party talk about what workers *are* – their words on each occasion serving to confirm over and over again the extent to which workers are not revolutionary, since the mere fact *that it is possible for the former to say this* furnishes empirical proof of their

[*] On 4 March 1972. Pierre Overney, a worker at the Renault automobile factory at Boulogne-Billancourt outside Paris, was killed by security guards there on 26 February 1972. (Translator's note)
[**] Secretary-general of the *Parti Communiste Français* from 1972 to 1994. (Translator's note)

analysis. Within the same sphere of bourgeois methodology, albeit far crazier in outlook, the Maoists believe that workers are totally and utterly revolutionary – and along grotesque Maoist lines to boot! – besides, they have a genuine desire to help the workers do just that: as in the Canton of 1927.* An understanding of what workers 'are' is in no way the historical problem here though – they are at the present time *merely workers* – the problem lies rather in understanding what they are going to become. This future evolution represents the sole truth of the proletariat's being, and the only key to a genuine understanding of what workers already are. To cite but one case in point, an important phenomenon is currently taking place that not only continues to escape the attention of professional commentators and nearly every single militant, but also promises them bad times ahead: as in the nineteenth century, workers *are starting once more to read*, and in the process will themselves come to understand the meaning of their actions. Despite being helpless in every respect and fully intending to remain that way, some antediluvian supporters of workers' control have criticised the SI for applying a strategy in May 1968. It is true that our action was firmly in accordance with certain strategic aims, but we in no way intervened *simply on our own behalf*. We did so on behalf of the movement that was there to hand, and at no point during it did we mislead anybody. This movement failed, or so we will be told. But then we never claimed that there was any

* In 1927, the attempt to set up a workers' government in Canton was crushed by Chiang Kai-shek. (Translator's note)

likelihood of it meeting with instant success in France – something that our writings of the period also bear witness to – whereas all the wonder-struck novices of the 'university revolution', viz. the likes of Alain Geismar and Jean-Louis Peninou, thought they would be able to spend the next ten years jabbering away among the furnishings of power.

Besides, it had some chances of success; and when *such a movement* has begun, it becomes essential to stay with it by employing the full range of one's ready skills within it. Far and away the most important thing to our mind, though, was that the May movement did succeed. We wanted to see it make at least half the number of inroads that it made, and this would have already constituted a triumph on a *global* level. The aftermath has proved us right.

As for Vaneigem, he recently jumped at the sorry opportunity of an introduction to selected extracts by Ernest Coeurderoy,[*] who for his part can do nothing about it, to try quite arbitrarily to infuse them with his opinion on revolution. It may be deemed the typical piece by the *common pro-situ* who has nothing to say but who wants to see his name in print; indeed, who would like to get the best price for the meagre promotional worth of his name on the *wrapper* adorning somebody else's book. However, in order that he actually see his name in print, he also needs to talk independently on issues that are beyond him. So much so that not only the hollowest turns of phrase

[*] Ernest Coeurderoy (1825–62) writer, socialist and later anarchist. Author of *Hurrah! Ou la révolution par les Cosaques*. (Translator's note)

going, but also long series of redundant concepts pile up any old how in what appears to be a bad *pastiche* of Vaneigem *circa* 1962. The spectacle, just like Vaneigem, seemingly owes the fact that it constantly gains in strength to the fact that it is continually getting weaker (and vice versa); and if, as ill luck would have it, we meet with no revolution, then we will be in for an ever-increasing number of terrorist confrontations between one group and another; he moreover drops a hint that the SI could well end up throwing in its lot with an extremism of the left-wing, truly fanatical variety. The hidebound, archaic abstractions he serves up do get a light sprinkling, however, of totally worthless 'theory'. He lays bare a certain conflict between the 'wealthy, ruling bourgeoisie' that he sees purely and simply in terms of 'technocrats, union leaders, politicians, bishops, army generals, high-ranking cops', and 'the poverty-stricken, exploited bourgeoisie with its departmental heads, low-ranking cops, small shopkeepers, down at heel clerics, executives', whence we begin to get a fair idea of just how rigorous and accurate his findings are. We come across another gem further on when he discovers that 'what weighs upon us is no longer capital, but the logic of the commodity'. He knows full well that Marx did not wait for him to demonstrate that capital was merely 'the logic of the commodity'; even so, he reckoned naively on his phrase *having a modern sound to it*. Thus in similar wise, thanks to a secret which this one-man-operated Vaneigemism has unearthed, we learn that what weighs upon us 'is no longer the power of a single individual or a class conscious of its predominance ...'. But who does he think will fall for this? The ruling class is everywhere just as *conscious of its predominance* as Vaneigem is himself conscious of his inferiority. By their very tone, these hastily cobbled-together revisions of his remind one not so much of Eduard Bernstein or even Edgar Morin, but of Louis Pauwels.[*] Like a more educated version of Henri Lefebvre, or a Jørgen Nash with less of the madcap swindler about him, thinking to make good his escape by *default*, Vaneigem comes out strongly in favour of the 'situationist project', in the hope that the reader will overlook the extent to which he has shown himself to be unworthy of such a project, and be unable to catch on straightaway to the fact that this recent handful of pages furnishes overwhelming proof of his unworthiness. The recalling to mind of two immensely significant details here will suffice to show the degree to which Vaneigem rides roughshod over his sorry readership (in order for it to keep going, weakness needs to assume that just about everybody is of an equal or greater weakness). Vaneigem briefly mentions in passing that by November 1970, the only thing that the SI was inspiring him with was 'indifference'. Foregoing any further explanation, he thinks he can pass the matter off as a *sudden mystery*. However, just as there is nothing mysterious about it, neither was there anything sudden (cf. report from the seventh SI Conference in 1966 appended to the present work). Furthermore, although he slips in the (for him)

---

[*] Louis Pauwels (1920–97), writer and editor. Founder of the journal *Planète*. (Translator's note)

rather cynical fact that 'there is no radical appropriation of theory so long as it is not experienced', he casually tries to reappropriate his usual sneaky bluff by showering praise on those who in May 1968 were 'the rebels of the will to live'. We have demonstrated that both during and prior to the occupations movement, the SI in fact comprised something less vague and more specifically historical. Nevertheless, the 'SI's Communiqué Concerning Vaneigem' of 9 December 1970 also reveals that Vaneigem's will to live was by then at something of a remove from this particular insurrection.

# Appendix 3
## Guy Debord's report to the seventh SI Conference in Paris (excerpts)

The SI's theory is at least clear on one point: *it must be put to use*. Already to the fore as a collective platform, and having no real meaning other than from the point of view of an immense, collective broadening of our critique, it forces us to come up with an answer to the following question: what have we actually *to do*, given the fact that we are together? This question is of very real importance, not only because the entire body of SI theory, being the complete opposite of an intellectual specialisation, covers a fairly large, complex network of elements possessed of varying degrees of importance; but *especially*, given that the basis of the agreement between us lies purely and simply on a theoretical level, because its entire validity depends in the last analysis on the way we understand and realise the use of this theory. What, for ourselves and towards others, should this common activity be? This question is one and indivisible. The wrong answer, that is, that we possess an immediate intuition of the totality and that this amounts in itself to a total qualitative attitude that enabled us to talk and write brilliantly about everything, would obviously be a pre-Hegelian demonstration of idealism because such a conception lacks both *seriousness and the work of the negative*. Our activity cannot be that absolute, that night in which all cows are radically black, which also means that *state of repose*. The fact that our shared understanding can remain partly inactive, and that individual activities can remain partly misunderstood by those who put up with them, is all in the same movement. If our judgement of the SI is wrong, then, as a consequence, we will be wrong about everything else. ...

This means that we must not become collectively bogged down in individual issues that elude our common activity; just as none of us need be troubled in his individual existence with the SI's collective *claims* that would lie beyond authentic common practice. I suggest that the existence of these abstract, collective positions should serve neither to gild such-and-such a person's inactivity nor to clutter up the actual life of any one of us. This presupposes of course that participation in a genuine, collective activity does in fact exist. This *practical* activity constitutes the only judgement our grouping recognises, just as this practical activity on the part of others will pass objective judgement on us.

It is plain that our common activity must become more broadly based. I propose only that we face the fact that, as it stands at the moment, this practical activity is a very long way from being adequate. We must admit to its limits and wretchedness precisely in order to provide it with a broader base in practice. On the other hand, the fact that it is subject to no *practical* assessment whatsoever enables it to appear grandiose. Yet such a grandiose appearance would be belied should a particular reckless practice of inactive relationships ever establish itself among us. I therefore consider that we have literally no reason to be together independently of an activity defined by our collective agenda (bringing the latter moreover into sharper focus). This activity is itself controlled not only by our place in the world but also by what we need to carry out both in terms of the critique of the modern world and the *conjunction* of critical elements appearing therein.

I am taking account here of a few discussions which have been going on between us, albeit rather sketchily, over the past few months. I am taking even more account of a few individual doubts which have at times displayed a kind of helplessness faced with those problems to do with the *practical expression* of the declarations we quite easily arrive at together. Two corresponding positions will more or less follow from this, and deserve to be highlighted immediately here:

1. A mock critique of the SI that would express unqualified dissatisfaction about the fact that the SI does not effect a magical transformation of every aspect of those people's lives who come into contact with it. The fresh-faced literary hack François George was a good example of this, going around criticising us for the SI's inadequacies.
2. Meretricious praise for the SI that I adjudge to be even worse because it already contains a kind of ideology of an *illusory power*. This praise would be an attempt to make people think that from the moment it 'comes into being', the SI *is already everything that it should in fact be* (in terms of coherence, etc.). Such an illusion

could as a consequence lead to absurd misconceptions about what the SI still ought to become, as a product of the imaginary basis with which it is credited nowadays. Both this praise and this denigration – the one moreover necessarily leading to the other – are two sides of the same coin: lack of understanding and absence in relation to the conditions of our real activity, and to the real possibilities for our activity.

The fact is that the weakness and the rudimentary nature of the new aspects of class struggle within modern society can, both around us and within our ranks, produce neo-idealistic expectations of an intellectual apocalypse, in relation to the SI as it actually exists; and, inevitably, disappointments in return, arising from the same expectations. The course of this struggle alone will transform the real problems, and the *false ones* too.

Our task first and foremost is to create an overall critical theory and (therefore inseparably) to *communicate* it to every sector already objectively involved in a negation which remains subjectively piecemeal. Further definition, experimentation and long-term work around this question of communication constitutes our most important, real activity as an organised group. The shortcomings *on this score* serve to sum up *all* our shortcomings (as a group). Everything else is mere chatter. ...

The revolt within real life right now and for us, rather than some theoretical guarantee of classical German philosophy, is the key to an understanding of both the critical culture that ran parallel with Marxism in its time (modern poetry as the self-negation of art, to cite but one example) and every form particular to the twentieth century, all of which need our concrete criticism, beyond a mere denunciation of commodity hype.

The full participation in what I call our main activity at its present stage of development obviously presupposes, as well as it reinforces, individual capabilities, both in terms of theoretical awareness and the present use of life. However, we can on no account be justified in putting forward a sophisticated analysis of abstract theoretical problems as *our collective task*, because our *theory of dialogue* must not be satisfied with a mere *dialogue of theory*: from its origin to the form it finally assumes, the theory of dialogue is a critique of society.

Contrary to what some people seem to think, *it is not that difficult to understand us theoretically*, once people are in contact with us and come to share our interpretation of the realities we are discussing. It is not *compulsory* to begin rereading Machiavelli and Kautsky. It must be easier to understand us now than it was, say, five years ago. ...

The difficulty therefore does not lie so much in acquiring a shrewd grasp of SI theories as *in putting them to some, even superficial, kind of use*. This indeed must now rank as our number-one priority.

The SI should therefore be careful not to have anything more to do with singing its own praises. There must be no further attempt to foster, both within our ranks and around us, an admiring complacency based on what we have done in the past (which, let's admit, amounts to both a great deal and very little); we must look instead at how we can put what we have done in the past *to use* now. We need to look too at the practical *abilities* of those people who sound us out. The various steps, including members' expulsions, that we have taken *to defend* the term 'situationist' have been taken solely in order to prevent it acquiring increased prestige *against us*. At no time has the aim been to increase its prestige in our eyes. We must call the whole nature of the movement we are gambling on to mind here.

The complex theoretical and practical activity which has its origin in this key aspect of advanced revolutionary *communication* in the broadest sense, can alone determine situationists' own mode of association, as well as every criterion that enables us to judge both the coherence and the abilities of our potential comrades. Bear in mind if you will that there is hardly any personal characteristic, even in relation to the most 'subjective' tastes and attitudes, that does not have a direct, measurable impact *on this whole area of our communication with the outside*. This is where, for example, the inability to communicate appears as a dangerous tendency to waver or as the dissemination of partial truths that turn into lies. This is also where the conformist bearing of one of us in any aspect of his own life could of course serve to discredit all the SI's theoretical claims; and all the more rapidly the more trenchant such claims seem. We must be *at least* at the level of the emancipation which is beginning to emerge just about everywhere without theoretical consciousness; and merely have theoretical consciousness *besides*. As clearly as we have to refuse the 'prestigious role' within the SI, we must reject whoever, both within our ranks and outside them, displays the opposite of prestige: *inadequacy* in relation to our stated principles.

It has recently been said that the situationists could not acknowledge any 'retired thinkers' within their ranks. This is quite true, because it would transform us into some intellectual guild for the dissemination and recognition of our 'masterpieces', and of the given doctrine that could be derived from it and thereafter taught. However I believe that this warning would have some of the characteristics of triumphant utopianism if we chose to put it forward as the chief danger. In the first place, because we are far more likely to bring together 'thinkers still in the cradle' (which is no bad thing on sole condition that they are out of the cradle soon). Above all though, and I wish very much to insist on this point, we in no way need 'thinkers' as such, that is, people coming up with theories outside practical life. Insofar as the theories we are in the process of formulating seem to me, both at present and in the conditions we have been facing, to be as sound as possible, I admit that any theoretical development that could fall within the coherence of 'situationist discourse' *comes from practical life*, emerging indeed as a legitimate consequence of it. However, this is very far from being sufficient. These theoretical formulations must themselves *crop up in practical life*, otherwise they are not worth 15 minutes' consideration. Consideration does however need to be given to the following two points: (1) the visible relationship between this theory and the life led by its bearer over the whole range of what can be accomplished in practice; (2) the use of this theory in so far as it can be communicated to those forces swept along in practice towards the search for this theory (wherever 'reality seeks its theory', as a time-honoured phrase has it). Deficiency in the first case plainly produces the thoughtless ideologue at odds with himself; and gives rise in the second instance to the utopian sect where real agreement admittedly exists between participants, but only among them. In our case, circumstances are further aggravated by the specific fact that we are proclaiming the historical refusal of ideology, as well as the transcendence of all utopianism by means of the real *potential* contained in the here and now. In both cases, the full extent of what can be accomplished, and thus of what is still wanting, can quite easily be established – and continually broadened – by situationists' actual practice if they effectively apply the basic banalities they already posit. ...

I reject both the sense of satisfaction or the threat of dissatisfaction about the SI that would emerge concerning the express demand to have us function as some kind of *holiday organisers*. There is no need for us to meet such a claim for *specific festivities*. We must leave this whole dimension up to the individual; that is, we should not throw an inevitably feeble collectivism about this kind of thing into anybody's path. What we need to inherit from modern art in the present circumstances is a deeper level of communication, and not a claim to some second-rate aesthetic enjoyment. ...

Our task is in no way to try and reappropriate 'cultural prestige' or some remnant of the latter, but *that promise* contained within culture. (We must protect ourselves against the 'prestigious roles' that SI membership could confer – along the wretched lines of those 'intellectual' or 'lifestyle gurus' currently on the scene – by systematically undermining any prestige-seeking attitude.) The search for some kind of festive activity in the SI would lead to the quite trivial practice of entertainment in society at large, which, although certainly no bad thing in itself, would be bad for us because this practice is shrouded in an ideology of playfulness: that is, an attempt at collective playfulness *without its means*, but made worse by a kind of doctrine of play. So where are all the immediate and future means to realise this playfulness? They are to be found entirely in our practice of communication with 'the real movement that abolishes the existing state of things'. Failing this, why, in such conditions of abstract ponderousness as currently obtain, should even a gathering of situationists be in any way entertaining?

In the alienation of everyday life, the opportunities for passion and playfulness to find expression are still very real, and it seems to me that the SI would be seriously in error were it to suggest that all life outside situationist activity was completely reified (which activity would thus be some conceptually mystical rescue job – witness a few people labouring under this impression who are currently sounding us out). On the contrary entirely, it seems to me that such free rein more often than not lies outside our collective activity, which latter entails a certain exhaustion. This seems even more obvious to me when one considers the personal theoretical work that participation in the situationist project can lead people to undertake.

Via an infinite number of interactions – nothing more than the comical, anecdotal side of which features in certain cases of spectacular plagiarism – the development of situationist theory has gone hand in hand with that of the dominant cultural sphere itself. Both the idea of unitary urbanism and the experience of the drift must today be understood in terms of their *struggle* with modern forms of utopian architecture, the Venice Biennales or *'happenings'*. In the same way, our possible use of a 'communication containing its own criticism' must come out against co-opted forms of neo-dadaism or against the cobbling together of neo-aesthetic alements (e.g. A 'Visual Art Group' constructing situations in the streets of Paris, etc.). The fact however that the few attempts which have been made to co-opt the SI as a whole into this cultural domain have been resisted, justifies these initial *moments* of our experience: we have been guided by the possibility of radicalisation that they contained. This is why the movement of supersession that we have been referring to does not abolish them. It is because of these very experiences – the pursuit of which will continue – that, rather than having anything to do with political activism, the task of *communicating* our theory (which I conceive to be our main practical link) is in fact radically opposed to all remaining vestiges of this specialist-led activism. However, the sole position that brings the necessary critique of specialists into total disrepute is *the inactivity in the name of the totality* that I referred to in my opening remarks.

The question of the communication of a theory in the process of formation to radical movements which are themselves in the process of formation (a communication that can in no way be unilateral) partakes at one and the same time of 'political experience' (organisation, repression) and of the formal experience of language (ranging from the critique of dictionary definitions to the actual use of books, pamphlets, journals, the cinema and the spoken word in everyday life). What we are faced with immediately afterwards here is the by-no-means-insignificant problem of finance. I take it that the problem of a minimum of creature comforts is an entirely insignificant one as far as all of us are concerned. It is certainly the case that wherever we are beginning in part to communicate what we want to say effectively, the result can come back to us in various uncomfortable forms – as with the firebomb at Martin's house. But the least insignificant problem of all is that of our ability in different circumstances to judge practical possibilities. Our envoy to Algeria for example had recently brought back some very optimistic conclusions regarding our prospects for a distribution network, without which even the best analyses are only fit to be deposited with the International Institute of Social History. What happened afterwards showed that he had been over-enthusiastic. Naturally, conditions of clandestinity reduce those among whom we must choose to place, or not place, our trust to a tiny number of individuals. According then to the precise nature of the latter's future activities, or lack of them, we can expect to achieve either results or nothing at all. You will nevertheless be *au fait* with the circumstances we all face *everywhere*, and this by the way is why I find this instance of a plot interesting. In our eyes, the whole world is like the Algeria I have been referring to, where everything depends on what we will be able to do with the *first individuals to come along*; and where we all need, therefore, to be increasingly capable of judging them in a practical way and of creating the conditions for such encounters. We have no *mass media*, and neither will any radical movement for a very long time to come. We will have to learn how to recognise and use other methods *at any time*.

If we are enjoying a certain theoretical lead at the moment, this is down unfortunately to the total absence of society's practical critique in the period we are now leaving, and to its subsequent theoretical decay. However, since it seems that the reappearance of struggles in new forms is beginning to offer confirmation of our basic theory, we need to communicate our positions to the new movements that are seeking to establish their identities both in politics and in culture, inasmuch as we are *their own undiscovered theory*. It seems to me that this task defines the whole of our present activity and vice versa, nothing can really be defined beyond it. Because, no more than it is a question of laying claim to a monopoly on critical excellence in any field whatsoever, we must not argue from the point of view of continued support for some monopoly on theoretical coherence.

(July 1966)

# Appendix 4
# Raoul Vaneigem's letter of resignation

Comrades,

The tendency that established itself in the French section on 11 November 1970 has the merit of being the last abstraction to be able to achieve expression within, on behalf and in the name of the SI. If it is true that the group has never been anything other than the very unevenly distributed abilities and weaknesses of its members, there is no longer at the critical moment we are now facing any discernible community, or even tendency, to make us forget that each and every one of us is alone in answering for himself. How did what was exciting in the consciousness of a collective project manage to become a sense of unease at being in one another's company? This will be for historians to establish. I feel no vocation, be it that of historian or intellectual, retired or no, to become war veteran, not to mention the fact that the straightforward analysis of the limited penetration of situationist theory into working-class life and of the limited working-class penetration into situationist life would at once merely be a pretext for the false, clear-cut consciousness of our failure.

Doubtless though, to get down at last to concrete matters – for there is no concrete response beyond the proof that everybody will have to furnish concerning what they truly are – I must talk instead here about my failure. As far as the past is concerned, I have always very rashly ascribed at least as many abilities and marks of honesty as I recognised in myself to the majority of SI comrades or former comrades, thereby labouring under as many illusions about others as about myself. I have a fair picture of what such an attitude has contradictorily managed to produce within the International in terms of manoeuvring tactics of the more or less clever and always odious kind, and create at the same time the conditions for ideology to emerge therein. Having said this, not only comrades' individual history, but also my own and that of the group will take my mistakes and my correct choices into account. (I wish nevertheless to make it perfectly clear that I spit in the face of whoever, either now or in time to come, would detect the presence of any secret intention whatsoever on my part, along moreover with that critical sincerity which we have so often seen go on display after the event.)

All I need do at present is recognise my failure to advance a movement I have always regarded as the very condition of my radicality. It would be disarming naivety itself to want still to rescue a group in order to redeem myself, when I have never in fact managed to turn it into anything approaching what I really wanted it to be. I prefer then to resume the gamble that my membership of the SI had postponed: disappear totally or rebuild my own coherence from scratch, and rebuild it on my own so that I may do so with the greatest number of people possible.

However, before leaving the job of recognising its own to the revolution, I am anxious from this day forth that the demands I set out concerning autonomous groups should also apply to me: I will resume relations with those comrades who wish to resume them, and whom I wish to see again, solely in the event of the actual triumph of the kind of revolutionary upheaval that my taste for radical pleasure will have managed to undertake.

Nevertheless, if the tendency judged its critique to be quite enough *per se*, with further proof unneeded, to reconstitute the French section, it should immediately regard me as somebody who has resigned, with the consequences I fully accept of never setting eyes on one another again.

(14 November 1970)

## Appendix 5
## Communiqué from the SI concerning Vaneigem

Finally obliged to go into serious mode and say something *specific* about what the SI is and what it needs to do, Raoul Vaneigem has immediately stepped in to reject it lock, stock and barrel. Up to now, he had always given *everything* to do with it his seal of approval.

His stand of the 14 November has the last-ditch and sad merit of giving clear and succinct expression to what was at the very heart of the crisis experienced by the SI in the years 1969–70. Although the view heatedly expressed by Vaneigem concerning the reality of this crisis is quite clearly upside down, his presentation is nevertheless an accurate one and, given this degree of visibility, the fact that it is standing on its head is unlikely to get in the way of interpretation.

Vaneigem calls our position the 'last abstraction to be able to achieve expression within, on behalf and in the name of the SI'; and just as he had never so much as glimpsed any of the preceding abstractions, he wants at least to combat this one. It thus behoves us here to talk not only about what is concrete, but also about abstraction, and about who is discussing abstraction.

From the very beginning, the concrete background to this crisis has included a defence of the reality underpinning the SI's activity, and of the real conditions in which this activity has essentially been carried out. The crisis began when some of us caught on to, and started to publicise, the fact that others were sneakily landing them with the monopoly of responsibilities to be taken, as well as the largest share of the business to be transacted: the critique undertaken concerning the insufficient (quantitative and especially qualitative) participation in the drawing-up of our main collective publications spread quickly to the insufficient, more covert participation as regards theory, strategy, meetings, struggles outside our ranks and even day-to-day discussions, all bearing on the simplest decisions that it falls to us to take. What could be found everywhere was a whole category made up in fact of *contemplative* comrades regularly setting their seal of approval on everything and never displaying anything other than the strongest determination to do absolutely nothing. They behaved as though they fancied they had nothing to gain, but maybe something to lose by defending a personal point of view and by undertaking to work independently on any one of our *specific* problems. On those occasions it chose to disport itself, this position, whose main weapon was its unfailing silence, also received an overlay of a few sweeping proclamations invariably shot through with more than a hint of euphoria concerning not only the achievement of perfect equality within the SI, but also the radical coherence of its dialogue, and the collective and personal greatness of every single one of its members.

To the end, Vaneigem has remained the most remarkable instance of this kind of practice.

The moment when a combination of several months' debate and a number of decidedly unambiguous writings had brought the criticism of these shortcomings to a stage where it was no longer possible in all honesty for the individuals concerned either to go on deluding themselves or to believe they could still foster the same illusions in others, was also the point when, more than anybody else, Vaneigem retreated into silence. It was only when he learnt, on 11 November, that our positions would from now on be disseminated outside the SI that he judged there and then that it would no longer be possible for him to remain tight-lipped.

Having reached this point, the broadside Vaneigem then launches against us finds him referring to 'manoeuvring tactics of the more or less clever and always odious kind'. He is clearly however not going to get anybody to believe that it would be necessary to have a tactic, or to be 'more or less clever', or indeed to engage in any kind of manoeuvring at all, in order to oblige a comrade who, for so many years had belonged to an organisation run along continually vouched-for egalitarian lines to take an effective part in the process by which that organisation on the one hand makes, and on the other carries out, its decisions; or to own up promptly to the fact that he cannot and will not. It may no doubt be possible for Vaneigem's, or indeed other people's, absence and silence to remain veiled for some time by means of manoeuvres characterised to a greater or lesser degree by pettiness, yet the former are quite easily eliminated the moment anybody at all makes it known that he or she will no longer put up with them, whereas for its part the contemplative position has to admit that there is really nothing in the world it hankered after more than the enjoyment of its continued toleration amongst us. But Vaneigem is using a plural that conjures up a past where such manoeuvres – 'of the always odious kind' to quote a phrase – were not yet aimed at him or his current imitators. We will not merely issue a reminder here that Vaneigem, having at no time raised, either in writing or at any meeting, or even – as far as we know – in the course of any discussion with a member of the SI, the slightest objection to any of these alleged 'manoeuvres', indeed having never in any way brought up their existence or for that matter the possibility that they might exist, is inexcusably and wretchedly *party* to them. We will of course go further: we absolutely defy him, before the judgement of the entire body of revolutionaries already in existence at the present time, to specify right now *a single one* of these 'manoeuvring tactics' he claims to have noticed, and somehow overlooked, in the SI during his decade-long membership of it.

Vaneigem, who pretends to believe that the SI is going to disappear because his absence will necessarily cause it to fade away ('to want still to rescue a group', 'to reconstitute the French section'), mentions that he has never managed to turn this group into 'anything approaching what [he] really wanted it to be'. We have no doubt whatsoever that Vaneigem wished to turn the SI into not only a revolutionary organisation, but one imbued with an altogether sublime, and maybe even absolute, excellence (cf. *Traité de savoir-vivre**, etc.). Other comrades have for years been saying that the SI's real historical triumph was never going to go that far, and above all too often consisted of *avoidable* defects (their existence moreover turning the myth of the SI's wondrous perfection, in which hundreds of stupid spectators on the outside – along sadly with a few spectators among us – were wallowing, into something all the more unfortunate). Vaneigem though, having now *post festum* adopted this tone of the disillusioned leader who never 'managed' to turn the group in question into 'anything approaching' what he had in mind for it, forgets to ask himself the following blunt question: what has *he himself* ever tried to say and do in the way of argument or exemplary action to cause an even better SI, or one closer to his best *declared* personal tastes, to emerge? The fact is that Vaneigem's contribution to the furtherance of such aims amounts to *nothing*; although, as it turned out, being *nothing* was scarcely what the SI settled for! Faced with the evidence of what the SI *has actually done*, Vaneigem is now in the process of totally discrediting himself in the eyes of any individual able to think, by propounding in so childish a manner the disgruntled and ludicrous fiction that sees the

---

* Raoul Vaneigem, *Traité de savoir-vivre à l'usage des jeunes générations* (Paris, Gallimard, 1967); paperback edition, with a new preface by the author (Paris: Gallimard, Collection Folio, 1992); English trans. by Donald Nicholson-Smith, *The Revolution of Everyday Life* (London: Rebel Press/Scattle: Left Bank Books, 1983); rev. edn, with Vaneigem's 1992 preface (London: Rebel Press/Seattle: Left Bank Books, 1994). (Translator's note)

SI, as well as Vaneigem himself, in terms of a comprehensive catalogue of failure. Vaneigem has never wanted to recognise *a share* of failure in the SI's actions, precisely because he knew he was too closely linked to this share of failure; and because the remedy for his real shortcomings has constantly seemed to him to lie not in their transcendence, but in the straightforward, categorical assertion that *everything* was for the best. Now that he can no longer carry on in this vein, the share of failure whose existence he has little option but to acknowledge is, in defiance of all plausible explanation, abruptly presented as total failure, as the absolute non-existence of our theory and our action over the last ten years. This bad joke just about sums him up.

Vaneigem's decidedly sociological-cum-journalistic reference to 'the limited penetration of situationist theory into working-class life' merely comes across as a particularly silly detail in the course of this basic farce of a letter; the most ridiculous thing of all moreover being his sensational *discovery*, in the unexpected light of this Last Judgment of the SI marked as far as he is concerned by his departure, that none of the situationists works in a factory! For if Vaneigem had known about this earlier on, since he seems so much affected by it, he would of course have pointed out both the problem and some radical solution to it.

As it is, it should be recalled that back when he was serious, Vaneigem had not merely set forth the commendable aims he had in store for the SI. The one out of all of us who did by far the most talking about himself, his subjectivity and his 'taste for radical pleasure', also harboured commendable aims *for himself*. But did he in fact fulfil them, or even genuinely struggle for that matter to do so? Not in the slightest. For Vaneigem as well as for the SI, the sole purpose of the *action plan* drawn up by Vaneigem is to spare all the effort and little historical risks of *realisation*. The aim being an all-encompassing one, it is viewed solely in the context of an abstract present: it is *already there* in its entirety, as long as it is thought possible to give that impression, or else it has remained absolutely inaccessible: nobody has managed to do anything to define it or to get anywhere near it. The qualitative, just like the spirit animating séance tables, had given the impression that it was there, but it must be admitted that this was nothing but an error, and a long-drawn-out one at that! Vaneigem has at last realised that the final mix he pretended to be so pleased with is in fact all wrong.

It is certainly possible in such a metaphysical light to wait for the pure moment of Revolution to happen, and, in the course of this relaxing wait, kindly leave 'the job of recognising its own' to the latter (although 'its own' will however need to be able to recognise this Revolution too, in addition, say, to cancelling their pre-booked holiday arrangements, should the two things unfortunately happen to coincide). Nevertheless, when dealing with matters that lie in more immediate proximity to our consciousness and direct action, like the SI and Vaneigem in person, if claims are being made that everything hoped for has already been achieved in every single particular, then blind belief really has degenerated into *bluff*. There will therefore come a day when what was declared perfect will have to be declared non-existent – and what a delightful discovery that will be, one moreover that in no way affects Vaneigem's wholly extra-historical radicality. Illustration enough then, that by admitting here and now that he has totally misjudged the SI, Vaneigem is oblivious to his already tacit admission that he has totally misjudged himself. He thinks he is still in 1961, ten years having gone by like a mere dream, that minor bad dream of history to be precise, after which Vaneigem, ever true to form, rediscovers the project he once nursed but had purely and simply 'postponed' for 'rebuilding [his] own coherence from scratch'. However, if the SI has not yet happened, then neither has Vaneigem. Perhaps one day soon though, who can tell? Coherence can wait! But since historical justice, quite as much as real action within history, is alien to Vaneigem's concerns here, he can scarcely be said to be doing himself justice.

Vaneigem has occupied an important and unforgettable place in the history of the SI. Having rallied in 1961 to the theoretical and practical platform devised in the first years following the SI's inception, he then immediately went on to share in and develop the most extreme positions they contained, ones which *in those days* were the most original and which *were heading* towards the revolutionary coherence of our times. If at that point the SI's contribution to Vaneigem was plainly in no way negligible, furnishing him with opportunity, dialogue, a few basic theses and a field of activity in which to develop whatever authentic, profoundly radical desires and potential he had, it is also true that Vaneigem made a genuinely remarkable contribution to the SI: he possessed a great deal of intelligence and culture as well as great intellectual audacity, all of which was dominated moreover by the sincerest rage against the existing state of things. Vaneigem was touched at that time by genius because he had a consummate ability to go to extremes in everything he was able to do. Anything he was unable to do was down simply to the fact that he had not yet had the opportunity to tackle it personally. He was raring to go. The SI of the period 1961–64, a period as important for the SI as it was for the ideas underpinning modern revolution, was possibly more influenced by Vaneigem than by anybody else. This was the period in which he not only wrote the *Traité* and the other texts signed by him in the SI journal ('Banalités de base' [Basic Banalities], etc.), but took a major part in drawing up the collective unsigned texts which appeared in issues 6 to 9 of this journal, and a highly creative part in all the debates of the period. Should he at the present moment have forgotten all about this, he can rest assured that we have not. Too bad, however, if nowadays he prefers to turn his nose up at his own achievements, for the revolutionary generation which has come into being over subsequent years has already used them to its own advantage.

The early 1960s was to be the period in which the broad lines of the most comprehensive revolutionary agenda were drawn up. The revolution, whose return and new demands we were proclaiming, was at that time totally absent, both in terms of a truly modern theory and in terms of individuals and groups struggling in a very real sense within the proletariat using radical behaviour of a new kind in order to achieve wholly new objectives. A certain generalising tendency, a certain use of abstraction, or even on occasion the use of a tone of lyrical outrage were the inevitable products of these specific conditions, and even turned out to be not only necessary but also wholly justified and quite excellent in the circumstances. Ours was not a large group at that time, and Vaneigem was there, able and daring to say what we were saying. We did well.

As immense good fortune would have it, and to an increasingly visible extent, the development of modern society has not failed to follow the path we had seen it embark upon; and, in the meantime, the new revolutionary movement, which did not fail to emerge as a consequence, has either been appropriating much of our critique, partially arming itself with our theory (which was clearly continuing to develop and become more focused), or even managing to draw its inspiration from certain examples of our practical struggles. We needed to make more specific *analyses*, and experiment also with various forms of action as and when they became possible. The situationists, in concert with their own times, became part of those increasingly concrete struggles that were intensifying in the period up to 1968, and have continued to gather momentum ever since. By this time however, Vaneigem was more conspicuous by his total absence.

'How did what was exciting in the consciousness of a collective project', we now find him wondering, 'manage to become a sense of unease at being in one another's company?' *He is nevertheless very careful not to answer* his question, which for this reason remains a purely elegiac one. How did pure gold turn itself into a base lead? In this instance it is quite simply because the consciousness of a shared project has ceased to exist in a shared practice – in what the SI's shared practice was actually *becoming*. Some were indeed living out the SI's practice, along with its difficulties and drawbacks, the worst of which was no doubt having to struggle against the creeping paralysis introduced into our shared activity by the contemplative and self-admiring tendency common to several situationists (cf. 'The Organisation Question for the SI', a text from April 1968 reprinted in issue no. 12 of the SI journal). On the contrary, all Vaneigem was perpetuating was the pure 'consciousness' of the abstract general nature of the project; and thus, as actions of real significance became more widespread, came to perpetuate not only an increasingly outmoded and deceitful consciousness, but also false consciousness within the so-called field of shared historical consciousness itself, to say nothing of dishonesty pure and simple. Under these conditions, it became less and less exciting to meet up with Vaneigem (and others who, for their part, had never even managed to excite anybody). Vainly repeating the same criticisms, only then to tire of doing so, is unlikely to go down well with anybody. This in addition to the fact that it must have been even more tiresome for Vaneigem to have to carry on, year after year in a completely different style, meeting comrades whom he knew full well were *very nearly as conscious as he was himself* of his failings. Nevertheless, by playing on the well-tempered vestiges of a friendly dialogue, and by turning a deaf ear, Vaneigem elected to keep up a nominal presence among us, one that rested on the memory of a once authentic participation and the ever more rcmote, more abstract promise of future fulfilment. The président de Brosses* had this to say about a similar sort of character: 'One cannot resolve to harry a close colleague, a truly good man of such a gentle disposition that he never utters a single word in reply to anything anybody may say to him. The problem is that gentle souls are the most obstinate and insensitive of all. They never take issue with you over anything. Yet neither will they be persuaded, nor prevailed upon.'

The years 1965 to 1970 were ones in which Vaneigem's eclipse became noticeable quantitatively (apart from three short pieces in the last three issues of the SI journal, he scarcely contributed anything at all to our publications over this period, and tended as a rule to keep quiet on those rare occasions he actually put in an appearance at a meeting) and above all qualitatively. His highly infrequent contributions to our discussions were characterised on the one hand by a consummate inability to envision real historical struggles, and on the other by the most wretched pussyfooting over any relationship to be maintained between one's words and deeds, and even by a cheerful obliviousness to dialectical thought. The seventh SI Conference in 1966 found us having to argue for two hours against an odd proposal put forward by Vaneigem: he was quite sure that our 'coherence' would, *in any debate concerning a practical task to be undertaken*, and after in-depth discussion, always denote the one, clearly recognisable in advance, true path. So much so that, were the outcome of the discussion to see a minority of situation-

---

* Président Charles de Brosses (1709–77) historian and statesman, president of the Dijon Parliament. (Translator's note)

ists not declare themselves totally convinced, the said minority would thus have proved that either it was not blessed with the SI's coherence, or it was dishonestly harbouring secret plans to put a spanner in the works, or at least an undercover theoretical and practical opposition. If the other comrades obviously defended the rights and duties of any minority within a revolutionary organisation – as witnessed by umpteen concrete examples – and even more simply the rights of reality itself, it must nevertheless be admitted that at no time since has Vaneigem ever ventured to contradict himself *on this point* by running even a ten-minute risk of being regarded as the holder of a 'minority' view on so much as the slightest discussion by the SI. The end of 1968 saw us go against Vaneigem's view on the matter and recognise the right, if need be, to set up tendencies within the SI. Vaneigem readily concurred in this majority decision, while making it nevertheless clear that he could not even begin to imagine how such a thing as a tendency would ever see the light of day among us. In the spring of 1970, a tendency having formed for the purpose of bringing about a quick and clear-cut resolution to a practical conflict, Vaneigem then decides of course to throw his weight behind it there and then. One could go on multiplying the examples but what is the point?

The permanent refusal to envisage a real historical development, engendered by his recognition and his *acceptance* of his own relative incompetence (which thus went on going from bad to worse), was usually accompanied in Vaneigem's case by enthusiastic insistence on every possible gross distortion of totality in the revolution as well as in the SI, and on the magical union at some future point between spontaneity unleashed at long last (not only the masses' but Vaneigem's too) and coherence: in such a marriage of identification, the ordinary problems to be met within society as it really is and in revolution as it actually unfolds will be instantly abolished *even before they have become an unpleasant topic for discussion*, which is obviously a nice prospect for the philosophy of history at the close of its proceedings. Vaneigem has been handling the concept of the qualitative by the ton while steadfastly overlooking what Hegel, in his *Science of Logic*, called 'the truth and the essential nature of things', *contradiction*. 'For as against contradiction, identity is merely the determination of the simple immediate, of dead being; but contradiction is the root of all movement and vitality; it is only in so far as something has a contradiction within it that it moves, has an urge and activity.' Apart from a brief period at the very beginning, what Vaneigem cared about was not the SI's life but its dead image, a glorious alibi for his own nondescript existence and abstractly sweeping expectations for the future. In view of the fact that he made himself perfectly at home with such a figment of the imagination, it is easy to see why 14 November 1970 found him totally dispelling it at a single stroke, just when he had perforce to start voicing his dissatisfaction, because the stance of smug silence could no longer be maintained.

At no point of course have we ever made the slightest suggestion that Vaneigem may have had 'secret intentions'. Our 'Declaration' of 11 November is far from being devoted to Vaneigem alone; and he knows full well that shortly before its promulgation, the American situationists had sent us within the space of a few days *three letters totally contradicting each other*, none of which, moreover, deemed it necessary to quote or amend what the one before it had to say; a state of affairs that leaves us with no option but to theorise about these comrades' 'hidden agenda', since the idea of their mental retardation is not one to which we subscribe for a moment. On the other hand, every facet of Vaneigem's conduct amongst us has always been both familiar to everybody and characterised beyond a shadow of doubt by an *ill-fated openness*. The whole question – albeit one decreasing in importance as time went on – centred on whether what so frequently earned Vaneigem criticisms and laughter within the SI would eventually be overcome, or carried on to the very end. We now know the answer. Vaneigem (and this goes for everybody else as well) was certainly not taken unawares by a debate, several of whose accompanying texts – about which nobody ever expressed the slightest reservation – had for months been asserting that not only was it of decisive importance, but that bringing it to a close had become a matter of some urgency, and that it was incumbent on all concerned to take a stand, knowing that the whole of our collective activity was being brought into play. Neither has Vaneigem anything to fear from that 'critical sincerity which so often we have seen go on display after the event'. Moreover his irony here is out of place since we are well aware that there have been many cases of the abrupt and unexpected severing of ties, where the explanation for an individual's behaviour could only become clear to us after the event. We are even more aware of the fact that one of the rare uses of Vaneigem's radicality has *always* been to approve of exclusions from the SI as soon as they happened, and to have little compunction about trampling on individuals who, even up to the day before, he had never bothered to criticise. And what in the last analysis are we supposed to make of this anti-historical rage against the whole notion of wisdom 'after the event'? Should we not for example be offering a riposte to the ragbag of platitudes that Vaneigem has just thrown together in his letter of 14 November? Up to that point he had never breathed a single word about them to anybody. In the circumstances, it is fully incumbent on us therefore *after the event* to criticise a particular instance of sheer stupidity that it might have been altogether reckless of us to predict in all its detail prior to Vaneigem's last heroic deed.

'The coherence of critique and the critique of incoherence are one and the same movement, condemned to decay and freeze into ideology the moment separation is introduced between different groups of a federation, between different members of an organisation, or between the theory and practice of one of its members' (Vaneigem, in issue 11 of the SI journal). There could be no better way of putting it; and there could hardly be a more impudent manner of exposing in a haze of abstract universality the very same imperfection one suffers from oneself in order to give the impression that *just because you have comprehensively denounced it*, it is obviously not something of which you yourself could be accused. Vaneigem was not unaware that his comrades would not, in the last analysis, *cover up* an imposture of this kind, despite the fact that treasured memories and the remains of a doting friendship based on them can temporarily delay the conclusion that even the slightest clear-headed assessment of, first every detail, and then the very heart of the problem calls for. We are not in the business of claiming to be sure of anything or anybody. Only of the movement of history, as long as we can recognise it by taking part in it; and no doubt each and every one of us claims to be sure on the subject of himself, at least as long as we are *capable of proving it*. It is in any case obvious that real and necessary *complicity* in an undertaking like the SI could never be based on a community of defects, and on the 'common project' of dazzling a whole host of followers from a distance by means of the trite and preposterous image of our collective splendour: we have always unanimously agreed that these people should be turned away and this image denounced, but it is not possible to see this task in any real sense through to a proper conclusion while *within the SI itself* this attitude of meek and woolly effusiveness, this *pietism of the SI*, was in fact present, without even the excuse of ignorant aloofness. The comfortably upbeat notion of participants' *complementary nature* was thus, 'with further proof unneeded', left to assert itself within the SI in an unduly exaggerated manner. Each participant found himself again and nobody got lost, since a few speciality acts had their place in the sun: the Nicolas Chamfort of the totality, the loyal drunk, the thrower of the best-intentioned cobblestones in the world, etc. It was here that absence became a policy of peaceful coexistence, and approval a necessity which passed itself off as a chance happening. And this is where Vaneigem has disappointed, if not himself the most – he's seen worse – then at least his comrades.

How did the contemplative situationists imagine – genuine as their willingness may be in this respect – that they were going to struggle against the hierarchical follow-my-leader attitude that became discernible *all around the SI*, and which we did so much to reject and condemn, when the fact was that they themselves, with some abstract and declared aim to foster egalitarian participation as their sole adornment, were to all intents and purposes followers *within the SI?* At this point, contempt for those followers on the outside became in point of fact *an imaginary confirmation of internal equality.* However, this 'follow-my-leader attitude' needs to be understood in its true complexity. Neither Vaneigem nor the others have ever been servile approvers of any policy that they in actual fact disapproved of: only Vaneigem's latest piece of writing very unfairly puts this image of himself before the public. In reality, Vaneigem and other comrades have always gone along with the decisions taken in the course of the SI's practice because they genuinely agreed with them and, we would hazard – as long as revolutionaries who are either more consistent than us or else placed one day in more favourable conditions than us to understand both the strategy we pursued and others that might have been possible, have not spotted our real mistakes – *because these decisions were right for our collective project.* Ever one to take an extremely firm stand against our enemies, Vaneigem has, on the other hand, never done or even contemplated doing anything over the course of the last ten years that in any way conflicts with the radicalism of the

SI's declared activity. All he has done is *make a very poor contribution* to the practice of this radicalism. Vaneigem seems never to have wanted to face up to the simple fact that it behoves anybody with such a mastery of language *to have some kind of involvement* in a number of analyses and practical struggles, for fear of turning out a complete and utter failure. Neither the vehemence nor the *de facto* views of the SI as a partial community could release him, though, from the obligation of making his own vehemence and *de facto* views plain on a number of concrete occasions. The care that Vaneigem had long been taking to distance himself from our activity tended to blind him to the existence of many of the relationships in this activity that were in actual fact of a hierarchical nature, relationships that his own escape mentality both accepted and encouraged. However, this very stance of aloofness was specifically adopted *in order not to see* this state of affairs, rather than helping to overcome it. After trusting the SI to act as the radical guarantee of the private life he was putting up with, he got to the stage where his conduct in the SI mirrored to an exact degree that of his own life.

Thus the *Traité de savoir-vivre* became part of a subversive movement of which the last has not yet been heard, at the very same time that its author bowed out of it altogether. He spoke only to melt into thin air. Yet the importance of this book should not be lost on anybody, for nobody, not even Vaneigem will be able to escape its conclusions in the fullness of time. As soon as Vaneigem let the old world gain the upper hand on him, the project he had believed in turned into *exorcism*, the vulgar sacralisation of a daily routine that, ever recognising the highly unsatisfactory nature of what was being countenanced, had all the more need to establish itself in the clouds of a spectacular radicality as an independent realm.

Sadly, it would appear that the totality is the fount of all comfort and support for his determination to put up with anything and everything, even to the extent of pretending to pass highly favourable judgement on just about everything. Apart from his strongly affirmed, definitive opposition to the commodity, the State, hierarchy, alienation and survival, it is plain to see that Vaneigem is somebody who has never rebelled against *anything* to do with the specific misery his own life was made into, the people around him and the people he chose to mix with – taken ultimately to include everybody in the SI. This curious timidity prevented him from confronting what he found unpleasant, but obviously not from being deeply affected by it. He sought therefore to protect himself by being constantly on the move, dividing up his life into several fixed temporal and geographical zones between which a kind of freedom to take the train still enabled him to ply. He has thus been able to console himself for a certain number of irritations endured just about everywhere, by means of whatever few trifling bits of revenge that such a frequently lampooned radical importance as his may get to wreak, and other little pieces of childish impudence, all politely covered up moreover by a sweet smile: keeping others waiting by turning up a bit late, repeatedly overlooking a tiny detail he was meant to see to, leaving a few people he had arranged to meet totally in the lurch and playing, or so he imagined, hard to get. These antics have enabled him to go a little way towards offsetting the unhappy consciousness of never really becoming the Vaneigem of his dreams, of constantly drawing back from adventure or even discomfort, not to mention the hunt for quality among people and moments; in a word, of failing to fulfil his desires, after expressing them so well.

Without a shadow of doubt, nothing could provide a more striking instance of the disastrous separation between theory and practice that his whole life illustrates – to the point of having fast sterilised his abilities as a theorist – than the following anecdote. On 15 May 1968, Vaneigem, who the day before had only just arrived in Paris, countersigned the circular entitled 'To Members of the SI, to the Comrades who Have Come Out in Favour of our Ideas', which called for immediate action on the most radical basis of what in two or three days time would become the occupations movement. This circular sought to analyse the course of events during the early part of May, outlined our involvement there and then (with particular reference to the Sorbonne Occupation Committee), studied the imminent possibilities of a crackdown and even the likelihood of 'social revolution'. The first factory occupation had in fact begun the day before, by which time moreover it would have been impossible for even the dumbest member of the most backward grouplet to harbour any doubt that a social crisis of the most alarming proportions had erupted. However, as soon as he had appended his signature to our circular, Vaneigem in his infinitely greater wisdom went off that very afternoon to catch the train back to his resort in the Mediterranean, and the holiday that had been arranged quite some time before. A few days later, getting wind abroad through the *mass media* of what was continuing as planned in France, he naturally set about returning, travelled with great difficulty the length of a France hit by strikes, and caught up with us again a week after his ludicrous *faux pas* just when the decisive days that had seen us able to do the most for the movement were already over. Now, we are well aware of the fact that Vaneigem has a sincere love of revolution, and that absolutely the last thing he lacks is courage. It is therefore impossible to grasp all this other than as a borderline case of separation between the strict routine of an unshakeably well-ordered everyday life, and a real but decidedly unarmed passion for revolution.

Now that he is shorn of the alibi of SI membership, since Vaneigem continues as loftily as before to broadcast the aim of putting the finishing touches to his coherence on foot or by car, on his own or 'with the greatest number of people possible', he should from now on expect those who will mix in his company and not be stupid – no doubt a minority – to ask him every so often *how, where, by doing what, and by struggling for which particular points of view* he is going to bring that famous radicality and his remarkable 'taste for pleasure' into play. There can be little doubt the pleasing silence that spoke volumes about the mysteries of the SI will no longer do; and his answers are going to be interesting in the extreme.

We have taken the opportunity here of coming up with a serious reply to what was very clearly no longer so. This is because we are continuing for our part to see to the theoretical tasks and practical conduct of the SI and because, from this angle alone, all the foregoing has its importance. An era has ended. It is this real change, and not some bad mood or impatience on our part which has compelled us to bring down the curtain on an established fact, and to break with a certain situationist conservatism which has for too long displayed its force of inertia and its sheer determination to self-replicate. We no longer want either Vaneigem or whatever could aspire to copy him within our ranks, or for that matter other comrades whose participation in them has amounted almost solely to formalistic play in the organisation, futile correspondence 'between sections' regarding bits of trivia, slight differences and false interpretations upheld and retracted across continents, followed six months later by further exchanges regarding the simplest decisions taken in ten minutes by those who, being there, had direct experience of the matter at hand – while compared with all this, the very same comrades' actual involvement in our theory and in real activity amounts to no more than a barely perceptible gesture. Revolutionaries who are not members of the SI have done far more to disseminate our ideas (and even, as has happened a few times already, to develop them further), than sundry die-hard 'situationists'; and without ceremoniously parading their 'quality' as the latter. We will once again prove that we are not playing at being the *management* of the new revolutionary movement, by shattering the ridiculous myth of the SI, both within its ranks and outside them, in the most direct way possible. We prefer the SI's real activity, in the here and now as much as in the past. And the reality of the revolutionary era we have become part of stands even more as *our real victory*.

An outdated academic style currently sees Vaneigem pretending he would rather 'historians' judge the actions in which he took part. It seems therefore to have slipped his mind too that it is not 'historians' who do the judging, but history, that is, those who make the latter. As long as they have not been wholly devoured (as a friend of ours used to say long ago), professional historians merely tag along behind. It therefore follows that on this matter, as on a few others, all historians of the future will do is confirm the SI's judgement.

(9 December 1970)

# Appendix 6
## Declaration of 11 November 1970

The crisis that has continually deepened in the SI in the course of the last year, and whose roots go much further back, has ended up revealing all its aspects; at the same time as it has produced an increasingly dire set of consequences in the shape of the replacement of theoretical and practical activity by an ever-more catastrophic tendency to sit back and do absolutely nothing. However, the most striking thing about this crisis (finally lifting the lid on what was precisely its original hidden centre) has been the *indifference* of several comrades in the face of its month on month concrete development. We are well aware that nobody has to any degree *expressed* this indifference. And this is the heart of the whole problem, for we can see only too well that, beneath all the abstract declarations to the contrary, what was actually being experienced was indeed a specific refusal to take any responsibility at all where participation in both decision-making and the implementation of our *real* activity were concerned; even at a time when the latter has seemed to be in such obvious jeopardy.

Considering at the same time that the action carried out by the SI was at least for the most part not only correct, but of major importance to the revolutionary movement in the period that came to a close in 1968 (with nevertheless a share of failure for which we need to provide an explanation); that this action *can* still have a significant part to play in this respect by developing a lucid understanding of the conditions in the new period before us, including its own conditions of existence; and that it is simply not possible for the dire position in which the SI has found itself for so many months to last any longer – we have established a tendency.

This tendency seeks to break completely with *SI ideology* and its result: the ludicrous conceitedness that both covers up and maintains inaction and incompetence. It aims to establish a precise definition of the SI organisation's collective activity and of the democracy that is *actually possible* within it. It wants *the concrete application* of this democracy.

After all we have seen over recent months, we reject in advance *any abstract response* that might still attempt to sham laid-back euphoria by finding nothing specific to criticise in the functioning – or in the non-functioning – of a group in which so many people know full well what their shortcomings were. After what we have for months been seeing with regard to the whole issue of our common activity, there can be no further acceptance of anything that has previously obtained: routine optimism becomes a falsehood, the unusable, abstract general nature of things a subterfuge. A number of the best situationists are turning into *something else*, people who are not talking about what they know and who do not know what they are talking about. We want to bring a radical critique to bear – a critique *ad hominem*.

Without wishing to prejudge any response of a more considered, serious nature that they may have to make at some future point, we hereby proclaim our disagreement with the American comrades who have established a tendency built on nothing but sand. At the present time the childish levity of pseudo-criticisms is as unacceptable a bluff as the dignified general nature of pseudo-contentedness; all of it being in much the same way an evasion of real criticism. For months now, other comrades have at no time ever ventured to come up with any kind of reply to what are clearly burning issues accumulated *by the facts themselves* and by the preliminary, *increasingly specific*, written criticisms that we have been formulating for months. The actual terrain of the scandal and its condemnation *have been expanding together* and any silence on the matter indicates the degree to which one is a *close party* to all these shortcomings. Let nobody, however, put our motivation down to naivety, as though this were an attempt here to launch some new tirade aimed at leaving a mysterious and crippling inevitability behind – a tirade that would meet with the same absence of response as all the ones before it! We are well aware that some members have felt no inclination to reply.

An immediate stop is going to be put to this shameful silence because *we demand*, in the name of the rights and duties that the SI's past and present confer upon us, that each and every one face up to his responsibilities here and now. It would be an utterly pointless exercise indeed were we to begin reminding everybody what the main issues awaiting resolution are. Every single one of us is aware of them – and they have even already been drawn up in writing. We need only add that we will of course not accept any reply that contradicts the actual existence of the person who frames it.

If some members have *hidden* aims different from ours, we want these aims to be brought into the open and to be expressed, as should of course be the case, in clearly defined actions carried out in accordance with clear-cut responsibilities. Should anybody moreover *not* have any real aims in mind, odd though the whole idea of anybody striving to preserve the *misery of yore* may appear to us, let's just say that we cannot and will not be a party to covering for some glorified, pseudo-community of 'retired intellectuals' or unemployed revolutionaries.

Our tendency is sending the present declaration to all the current members of the SI without distinction or exception. We wish to make it crystal clear, however, that we are not seeking to exclude anybody (and much less make do with excluding some scapegoat or other). But since we consider it highly unlikely that any genuine agreement can be reached *at such a late stage* with everybody, we are prepared for any split whose dividing lines will be determined by the forthcoming debate. And we shall for our part do everything possible in the circumstances to make any such split take place under perfectly equitable conditions, particularly by upholding an absolute respect for truth in any future polemic, just as collectively we have all been able to uphold this truth in every circumstance in which the SI has acted to date.

Considering that the crisis has reached a level that can only be described as alarming in the extreme, we henceforth reserve the right – in accordance with Article 8 of the statutes voted at Venice – to make our positions known outside the SI.

Paris, 11 November 1970
Debord, Riesel, Viénet

# Appendix 7
## Statutes adopted at the Venice Conference on 30 September 1969 (excerpt)

### *Article 8*

On any theoretical or tactical question that has not met with general agreement during a discussion, each member is at liberty to maintain his own opinion (as long as there is no breach of practical solidarity). If the same problems and differences of opinion are met with on several successive occasions, members of the SI who find themselves in agreement on one of these options have the right to set about openly establishing a *tendency*, and to draft texts for the purpose of clarifying and upholding their point of view, until such time as there is a conclusive outcome (by reaching general agreement again, by a split or by the practical supersession of the discussion). Such texts may be circulated throughout the SI and may also appear in the publications of one or more sections. As a rule, a tendency bearing on a general tactical problem will itself need to be international in nature (thereby marking a division within several sections).

# Appendix 8
## The *détournements** in the *Theses on the Situationist International and its time*

Thesis 2: 'The Minister of the Interior in France and the federated anarchists of Italy' (*The Communist Manifesto*).

Thesis 3: 'revised' (cf. 'revisionism' within Marxism).
'the real movement that abolishes the existing state of things' (quotation from Marx).
'bad side' (quotation from Marx, *The Poverty of Philosophy*).

Thesis 4: 'everything that it could be' (Stirner).

Thesis 5: 'the icy extrapolation of scientific reasoning' (*The Communist Manifesto*:
'in the icy waters of egotistical calculation').
'into everybody's minds' (quotation from the SI).
'censored', 'repressed' (two Freudian concepts).
'the judgement of the world' (Hegel, *Weltgericht*).
'poses only the problem it can solve' (Marx: 'Mankind sets itself only problems it can solve').

---

* See appendix 9. (Translator's note)

Thesis 6: 'pure thoughtless negation' (Hegel).

'has detached itself from itself and established itself in the spectacle as an independent realm' (quotation from *The Society of the Spectacle*, thesis 22, a *détournement* of the fourth *Thesis on Feuerbach* [Marx]).

Thesis 8: 'we no longer can or for that matter want to continue as before. At the top, there is no longer any possibility of doing so' (Lenin).

'the first fruits of the supersession of the economy are not only ripe, but have begun to rot' (Trotsky, *Transitional Programme*).

Thesis 11: 'In short, this world has lost the confidence of all its governments; they therefore propose to dissolve it and set up another one' (Brecht, 'June 1953 Poem').

Thesis 12: 'Morals improve. The meaning of words has a part in the improvement' (Lautréamont, *Poésies*).

'mankind ... joyously detach itself from its past' (Marx).

note 5: 'The proletarian Mandate of Heaven has expired' ('The mandate of heaven has expired' is a traditional Chinese expression that accompanies popular uprisings against a worn-out dynasty).

'Bacchanalian revels in which no member is not drunk' (quotation from Hegel).

The list of *détournements* in the author's own hand on his copy of *La Véritable Scission dans L'Internationale* (Éditions Champ Libre) ends here.

# Appendix 9
## *Détournement*[*] as negation and prelude
## (Guy Debord in issue no. 3 of the SI journal, excerpt)

Diversion or *détournement*, the re-use of pre-existing artistic elements in a wholly new entity, has been an abiding trend within the contemporary avant-garde both prior to and since the establishment of the SI. The two basic rules governing *détournement* are the loss of importance of each diverted [*détourné*] autonomous element – to the extent that its original meaning may be lost altogether – and at the same time the organisation of another meaningful entity that gives each element its new impact.

The peculiar power of *détournement* clearly stems from the fact that it serves to enhance the vast majority of the

[*] In everyday French, *détournement* (n.m.) and *détourner* (vt.) carry the general sense of diverting something or somebody from their original course. Thus *détournement de fonds* [embezzlement], *détournement de mineur* [corruption of a minor], *détournement de pouvoir* [abuse of power]. *Détourner* (depending on the context): to divert, reroute, hijack, ward off, deflect, distract, turn away, turn (a weapon etc.) aside, to twist (words), to lead astray, to side-track, to misappropriate, to find a different use for something or somebody (from the one originally intended). Also *détourné* (adj.) [roundabout (adj.), indirect, circuitous, oblique. (Translator's note)

terms by fostering the dual presence within them of their former and new-found, instantaneous meanings – their dual substance as it were. *Détournement* is practical because it is so easy to use and because the possibilities for its re-use are endless. On the subject of the ease with which *détournement* can be used, we have already had this to say: 'The cheapness of its products is the heavy artillery that demolishes all the Chinese walls of under-standing' ('Methods of *Détournement*', May 1956). However, these points on their own would not justify recourse to this method that only in the previous sentence had been described as 'clashing head-on with every social and legal convention'. What then is the historical signifi-cance that *détournement* undoubtedly possesses?

'The capacity for *devaluation* accounts for the playful character of *détournement*', writes Asger Jorn in his essay 'Diverted Painting' [*Peinture détournée*] (May, 1959), and he goes on to say that all the elements of the cultural past must be 'reinvested' or disappear. *Détournement* thus reveals itself to be first and foremost the negation of the value underpinning all previous forms of expression. It comes to light and gathers momentum in the historical period that is witnessing the decay of artistic expression. At the same time, the attempts to re-use the 'divertible unit' [*bloc détournable*] as material for other entities denotes the search for a far greater construction, a new monetary unit of creation at a higher level.

# Index

Freund, Julien, 79n

*Garnautins, The*, 59, 98, 116
Geismar, Alain, 126
George, François, 132
*German Ideology, The* (Marx), 21, 81
Germany, 115
Gierek, Edward, 74n
*Gierek face aux grévistes de Szczecin*, 75n
Giudecca, la, 82
*Gli operai d'Italia e la rivolta di Reggio Calabria* (SI pamphlet [Italian section]), 110
God, 35
Gombin, Richard, 27–8, 77n
'Guerres et Paix' (Freund), 79n
Guillaume, James, 1
*Guy Debord* (Jappe), 4n
*Guy Debord and the Situationist International* (ed. McDonough), 4n
*Guy Debord, la révolution au service de la poésie* (Kaufmann), 5n

Hahn, Pierre, 74n
*happenings*, 139
Havana, 101
Heath, Edward, 75n
Hegel, Georg Wilhelm Friedrich, 6, 30, 73n, 77n, 158, 175–6
hierarchy, 65, 67, 164
history, 15, 25–6, 32, 35, 42, 49, 58–9, 61, 66–7, 69, 93, 98, 101, 109, 112, 122, 143, 152, 158, 161, 168
*History of the Council of Nantes* (Quillet and Schumacher), 73n
Holland, 115, 120
Horelick, Jon, 94
Hussein, King of Jordan, 85

ideology, 24, 32–3, 39, 52, 59, 62, 94, 100, 108, 132, 137–8, 143, 160, 170
ignorance, 61
illness, mental, 76n
*Il Reichstag brucia?* (SI pamphlet [Italian section]), 86
*Image-action de la société, L'/The Action-Image of Society: On*

*Cultural Politicization* (Willemer), 121
Imperial Indian Army, The, 104
inequality, 66
Informations Correspondance Ouvrières (ICO), 88
intellectuals, 7, 42, 71, 105, 108, 137, 142, 172
intelligentsia, 27, 45, 46
'International Brotherhood' (Bakunin), 108
*Internationale Situationniste, L': chronologie, bibliographie, protagonistes (avec un index des noms insultés)* (Raspaud and Voyer), 121
*Internationale Situationniste 1958–1969* (journal, ed. Mosconi), 4n, 18, 29, 74n, 80n, 92, 156
International Institute of Social History, Amsterdam, 87, 140
International Working Men's Association (London French Branch), 99
Italian Anarchist Federation (FAI), 103
Italian Anarchist Federation Tenth Congress (1971), 104
Italy, 6, 16, 19, 103, 105, 110, 112, 175
*Irish question, the*, 16

Jansenism, 34
Jappe, Anselm, 4n
Jordan, 84
Jorn, Asger, 115, 178
'June 1953 Poem' (Brecht), 176

Kádár, János, 118
Kathmandu, 53
Kaufmann, Vincent, 5n
Kautsky, Karl, 134
Khayati, Mustapha, 84–6
'King Mob', 3
*King Mob Echo: English Section of the Situationist International (Texts 1966–1970)*, 5n
Kiruna, 117
Knabb, Ken, 4n, 51n, 80n
Ku Klux Klan, 113

labour, 19, 44, 47, 50

Lautréamont, comte de (Isidore Ducasse), 18, 176
Lefebvre, Henri, 128
leftism/leftists, 15, 17, 27, 71, 86, 91–2, 100, 102–3, 105, 109, 111, 113, 123–4
  see also ultra-leftism
Le Monde 74n, 75n, 76n
Lenin, Vladimir Ilyich, 45, 48, 176
Leningrad, 7
Le Nouveau Planète, 74n
Le Nouvel Observateur, 74n, 77n
Letterist International, 1
Lin Piao, 15
London, Arthur, 118
Long March, the, 123
  see also Mao Zedong
Loyal Servant, The/Le Loyal Serviteur (Jacques de Mailles), 86
Lydon, John, 5n
  see also Sex Pistols, The

Machiavelli, Niccolò, 134
MacLaren, Malcolm, 3, 5n
Mairowitz, David Zane, 5n
management, 27, 50, 167
managers, 13, 44, 47, 49
Mao Zedong/Maoism/Maoists, 15, 27, 118, 124–5
Marat, Jean-Paul, 115
Marchais, Georges, 20, 124
Martin, Jeppesen Victor, 140
Marx, Karl/Marxism, 1, 4n, 20, 30, 45, 73n, 76n, 77n, 124, 127, 133, 175–6
Marxism–Leninism, 27
masses, the, 30, 62–3, 65, 68, 73n, 123, 158,
mass media, 20, 140, 160
  see also spectacle
May 1968, 10, 37, 77n, 78n, 115, 117, 121–2, 125–6, 129, 165
McDonough, Thomas, 4n
Memoirs (Cardinal de Retz), 81
Menshevik, 46
'Methods of Détournement' (Debord and Wolman), 178
Milan, 7, 113
'Minimum definition of revolutionary organisations' (SI text), 66

misery, 31, 80n, 90, 164, 172
Monaco, 109
Morin, Edgar, 128
Mosconi, Patrick, 4n
Moscow, 15
'Motherfuckers, The', 3
Mussolini, Benito, 112

Naples, 110
Nash, Jørgen/Nashism, 115–16, 128
Nechaev, Sergei, 108
negative, the/negation, 28, 35, 58, 73n, 131, 133, 178
neo-dadaism, 139
neo-fascism/neo-fascists, 101, 106
New York, 73n
Nicholson-Smith, Donald, 4n
Nixon, Richard Milhous, 15, 109

occupations movement, 11, 15, 52, 56, 78n, 121–2, 129, 165
'Old Man of the Mountain, The', 114
'On the Poverty of Student Life'/'De la Misère en Milieu Étudiant' (SI pamphlet), 51
organisation, 26, 37, 61, 63–6, 77n, 78n, 85, 100, 102–3, 107–8, 124, 139, 147–8, 157, 160, 167, 170
'Organisation Question for the SI, The' (SI text), 79n, 80n, 155
orientation debate, 2, 69, 78n, 87
Origins of Modern Leftism, The (Gombin), 27, 77n
Overney, Pierre, 124

Pannekoek, Anton, 27
Paris, 75n, 113, 116, 123, 139, 165, 173
Paris Commune, 45
parliament, 105, 156n
Parti Socialiste Unifié (PSU), 108
Pauwels, Louis, 128
Pavan, Claudio, 87
Peninou, Jean-Louis, 126
petty bourgeoisie/petty bourgeois, 48–9, 50, 52,
Phenomenology of Spirit (Hegel), 6
philosophy, 117, 133, 158
Pitt, William (the Younger), 110
plagiarism, 138